Fulbright Papers

PROCEEDINGS OF COLLOQUIA

SPONSORED BY THE
UNITED STATES – UNITED KINGDOM
EDUCATIONAL COMMISSION:
THE FULBRIGHT COMMISSION, LONDON

Volume 12

Education in the age of information
The challenge of technology

EDITED BY CARL PAYNE

Technological advances pose novel and important questions for the education system. In this important contribution to the debate on education policy leading educationalists, industrialists and public policymakers from both the US and the UK discuss how education must adopt and adapt to new technologies.

The contributors argue that young people need to be better equipped for an ever changing world. They explore how school curricula are being redesigned, and how teachers are being retrained to exploit technology in the classroom. They also discuss changes in higher education, especially the development of new courses and modes of learning in response to an increased participation rate. Behind these developments lies a powerful economic pressure – industry's urgent need for a more flexible and technologically minded workforce. The book argues for a new partnership between education and industry.

Readership: educationalists, teachers, trainee teachers and students of education; education policymakers

Carl Payne is Head of Computer Services at South Bank University, London

The Fulbright Programme of Educational Exchanges, which has been in operation since 1946, aims to promote mutual understanding between the United
States of America and other nations. It now operates in more than 120 countries, with forty-three bi-national commissions involved in its administration.
In the United Kingdom the Commission aims to offer qualified British and
American nationals the opportunity to exchange significant knowledge and
educational experience in fields of consequence to the two countries, and
thereby to contribute to a deeper mutual understanding of Anglo-American
relations and to broaden the means by which the two societies can further their
understanding of each other's cultures. Amongst its activities the Commission
promotes annual colloquia on topics of Anglo-American interest; the proceedings are published in this series.

Education
in the age of information
The challenge of technology

Edited by
CARL PAYNE

MANCHESTER
UNIVERSITY PRESS

IN ASSOCIATION WITH
THE FULBRIGHT COMMISSION, LONDON

DISTRIBUTED EXCLUSIVELY IN THE USA AND CANADA
BY ST. MARTIN'S PRESS

COPYRIGHT © THE US – UK EDUCATIONAL COMMISSION, 1993

Published by Manchester University Press
Oxford Road, Manchester M13 9PL, UK
and Room 400, 175 Fifth Avenue, New York, NY 10010, USA

Distributed exclusively in the USA and Canada by St. Martin's Press, Inc., 175 Fifth Avenue,
New York, NY 10010, USA

British Library Cataloguing-in-Publication Data
A catalogue record for this book is available from the British Library

Library of Congress Cataloging-in-Publication Data
Education in the age of information : the challenge of technology / edited by Carl
   Payne.
      p.   cm. — (Fulbright papers ; v. 12)
   Papers presented at a colloquim sponsored by the Fulbright Commission and
held in London, Nov. 25–27, 1990.
   Includes index.
   ISBN 0–7190–3587–2
   1. Technical education—Congresses.   2. Technical education—Great
Britain—Congresses.   3. Technical education—United States—Congresses.
I. Payne, Carl, 1947–. II. United States—United Kingdom Educational
Commission. III. Series.
T62.E33 1933
607.1′1—dc20   92-42834

ISBN 0–7190–3587–2 *hardback*

Phototypeset by Intype Ltd, London
Printed in Great Britain by
Biddles Ltd, Guildford and King's Lynn

Contents

Tables and figures

Contributors

DR JOHN ASHWORTH, Director, London School of Economics and Political Science

PROFESSOR GARY BENENSON, City College of the City University of New York, USA

SIR ADRIAN CADBURY, Founding Chairman for the Foundation for Educational and Business Partnerships

SIR JOHN CAINES, KCB, Permanent Secretary at the Department of Education and Science

DR SHEILA O. GERSH and PROFESSOR ALFRED S. POSAMENTIER, City College of the City University of New York, USA

DR RONALD K. GOODENOW, Digital Equipment Corporation and Clark University, Massachusetts, USA

PROFESSOR GEOFFREY HARRISON, Nottingham Polytechnic

DR ANNE-MARIE ISRAELSSON, Director, Teknickens Hus, Luleå University, Luleå, Sweden

E. STINA LYON, South Bank University (formerly South Bank Polytechnic)

RT HON BARONESS PERRY of SOUTHWARK, Vice Chancellor, South Bank University (formerly South Bank Polytechnic)

PROFESSOR SIR WILLIAM TAYLOR, Vice Chancellor, University of Hull

MR DAVID WOOLDRIDGE, Vice President and General Manager, United States Federal Government Division, Motorola Inc, USA

Foreword

This volume records the proceedings of the Fulbright Colloquium on Technology: the Challenge to Education which was held in London from 25 to 27 November 1990. Convened by Pauline Perry, Director of South Bank Polytechnic in collaboration with Bernard Harleston, President of the City College of City University, New York, the Colloquium was the twelfth in the series sponsored by the Fulbright Commission and brought together academics and industrialists from the United States of America, Sweden, Germany, Austria and the United Kingdom.

Such colloquia are held at least once, and possibly twice, a year on topics of Anglo-American interest and importance. They are designed to supplement the traditional exchanges of scholars and students undertaken by the Commission in support of its aim of encouraging Anglo-American cultural relations. Such exchanges between this country and America now total 11,000 since the Fulbright programme started in the United Kingdom in 1948.

The Commission was especially pleased to have been instrumental in mounting a colloquium on Technology: the Challenge to Education – an area which calls for discussion at the highest levels. The pace of change of technology continues to accelerate and, to make best use of what technology has to offer, education methods need to adapt in a fundamental way. Participants in the colloquium contributed much to the current debate on this question and their wide interests are reflected in this publication. The substance of the presented papers is fully recorded but, from lack of space, a number of the reports from the many wide-ranging and stimulating discussions that took place during the meetings have, regretfully, had to be omitted.

The opinions expressed are, of course, personal to the contributors and do not necessarily reflect the views of the Commission. Nevertheless, the Commission believes publication of the proceedings will be welcomed by a wide audience and will provide a valuable contribution to the current international debate on technology and its impact on education.

The Commission wishes to thank Pauline Perry and her staff at South Bank Polytechnic for hosting the event and Bernard Harleston and faculty at the City College of City University, New York for their active participation in the planning and execution of the Colloquium. The Commission acknowledges with gratitude the support and sponsorship given also by Apple (UK) Limited and Digital Equipment Corporation (USA).

John E. Franklin, *Executive Director*
United States-United Kingdom Education Commission
The Fulbright Commission, London

Abbreviations

A Level	General Certificate of Education at Advanced Level
ACFHE	Association of Colleges of Further and Higher Education
AEB	Associated Examining Board
BA	Bachelor of Arts
B.Ed	Bachelor of Education
B.Sc	Bachelor of Science
BTEC	Business and Technician Education Council
CAL	Computer Assisted Learning
CATE	Council for Accreditation of Teacher Education
CATS	Credit Accumulation and Transfer Service
CDT	Craft, Design and Technology
CFV	Communications, Film and Video
CET	Council for Educational Technology
CGLI	City and Guilds of London Institute
CNAA	Council for National Academic Awards
CTC	City Technology College
DES	Department of Education and Science
Dip.H.E.	Diploma in Higher Education
D.o.E	Department of the Environment
EATE	Enterprise Awareness in Teacher Education
FE	Further Education
FEU	Further Education Unit
FTE	Full Time Equivalent
GCE	General Certificate of Education
GCSE	General Certificate of Secondary Education
HE	Higher Education
HMI	Her Majesty's Inspectorate
HND	Higher National Diploma
INSET	In-Service Training of Teachers
IT	Information Technology
JANET	Joint Academic Network
LEA	Local Education Authority
MA	Master of Arts
MSc	Master of Science
NCC	National Curriculum Council
NLA	New Liberal Arts
O level	General Certificate of Education at Ordinary Level
ONC	Ordinary National Certificate

OND	Ordinary National Diploma
OU	Open University
PCFC	Polytechnics and Colleges Funding Council
Ph.D	Doctor of Philosophy
PICKUP	Professional, Industrial and Commercial Updating
SERC	Science and Engineering Research Council
STS	Science, Technology and Society
THES	The Times Higher Educational Supplement
TVEI	Technical Vocational Educational Initiative
UBI	Understanding British Industry
UFC	University Funding Council

[1]

Introduction

BARONESS PERRY OF SOUTHWARK

This book is the outcome of a Fulbright Colloquium entitled Technology: the Challenge to Education held at South Bank University (then South Bank Polytechnic) in November 1990. The Colloquium format – literally coming together to talk – has always been productive, and this particular gathering generated intellectual discourse of exceptional quality and value.

The book explores the challenge that developments in technology place on the education system and considers how the system, at all its many levels, needs to prepare itself for an ever-changing technological world. The challenges are considerable, for education must set itself the task of ensuring that technology is exploited for the benefit of mankind. It might be useful to reflect on how difficult it would have been to imagine the speed with which technology has changed our lives, had this book been written just a few years ago. Now much of this technology is taken for granted as we become increasingly dependent on computers, telecommunications and a whole spectrum of developments based on microelectronics which are making an impact on our lives.

Technology is a very broad word and a very broad concept. Translating it into the educational context is by no means easy, and the United Kingdom's National Curriculum starts from the simple but inspired concept of pupils' development of the essential skills of designing and making things, drawing particularly on the basic tools of mathematics and science. Inevitably, there is and will continue to be debate about the way in which existing subjects such as the former handicrafts, home economics and business studies can contribute to this simple central theme, but it is my belief that the more that clear definition is adhered to the more flexible and powerful the central position of technology within the curriculum will be. The challenge to education is to provide pupils with the core skills of designing artifacts which are both functional and attractive, together with the equally challenging practical skills of making such objects. No one can predict the future, least of all the artifacts which will be the technological developments of a period far ahead, when the pupils of today will be the workers of thirty and forty years on, but we can send out into the world young adults who understand how objects are made and designed, and with some of the skills necessary to contribute to an economy based on such developing technologies.

If the education system is to fulfil its most fundamental mission, and justify its function, our teaching and learning methods must adapt so that technology is used to its full potential in the process of education itself. This will contribute just as much as the content of the curriculum to providing the children in our schools with a sense of familiarity with and mastery of the technological world in which they live. Such a sense of mastery is the educational mission of each generation: each has had to find its own way of providing children with the survival skills they need for their own future, and the confidence to believe that they can cope with the changes which will come. For our generation, the rapidly changing technologies provide a more daunting challenge than can ever have been faced before: it is by our response to this challenge that the education of the 1990s and the new millenium must be judged.

There is probably no simple way in which the concept of 'design and make' can be defined in terms of the existing curriculum subjects. The common theme which runs through all the contributions to this book is that technology as a concept must cover the whole curriculum, while retaining a distinct and separate place, as an identifiable subject area in its own right. Certainly, the need for our young people to approach problem solving in a creative and imaginative way cannot be overstated but the 'design and make' concept requires the one element at which the British educational system, at least, has never been wholly successful: that is, the bringing together of intellectual knowledge and understanding with practical applications. Inherent in our culture, and it would appear in much of the American culture, is a bifurcation of status and tradition between the intellectual understanding of science and mathematical principles, and the practical applications of that understanding into the creation and manufacture of everyday objects. It is the convergence and integration of these two parts which is the heart of the concept of technology as a new area in the curriculum.

By itself, the development of practical 'making skills' as seen in too many of the former Craft, Design, and Technology (CDT) departments and indeed in the teaching of much home economics, is woefully inadequate. Just as inadequate though are the departments which provide for the most gifted children a very sophisticated understanding of the principles on which engineering or computing are based, without any appreciation of the bridge between the theory and the practice. Art departments have enabled young people to reach very high standards of decorative design and artistic endeavour, but have all too rarely applied this to the design of everyday objects which constitute the environment of our lives, and make our lives ugly or beautiful by their nature and design.

A new area of technology will need to draw on all these elements, and bring them together to reach standards which are theoretically and practically of a very high level indeed. Inevitably, information technology will play a major role in the development of this subject, simply because our current technology is based on the flexibility of miniaturised computers so extensively. It would however be disastrous if technology in the curriculum was seen to be a glorified form of computer studies or even information technology.

I reject very much the concept of technology as an opportunity to solve problems, with no intellectual understanding of why some solutions work and others do not. My fear is that without properly educated teachers, technology lessons may well turn into an exercise of throwing paper darts around, or floating plastic bottles on water, without the necessary education in the principles which make some solutions successful. The tools for problem solving are more than a process of random experiment: they are also the knowledge with which to find and apply the solution. Just as the intellectual and practical must be brought together in an integrated area of technology, so the process of thought and approaches to problem solving must be integrated with the technical and intellectual tools to produce solutions. This means that in the overall curriculum there must be an enhanced understanding of information technology, a sophisticated comprehension of materials science, and a grasp of engineering, science and applied mathematics for every child. We should not be satisfied until we can assure ourselves that in addition to these intellectual understandings, the next generation will have practical skills in working with wood or with metal or with glass, with textiles and with food stuffs, as well as keyboard skills in computing and, perhaps most often neglected, the practical skills of communicating to and working with teams of other human beings with different approaches and different expertise from one's own.

Higher education must also play its part. At South Bank our degree in Engineering Product Design requires students to design and make real engineering products from the first year of their course, expecting of them a very high standard of finished project, incorporating engineering and design principles, produced also, incidentally, in a form which would be marketable at an appropriate price. Similarly, our degree in Consumer Product Management allows students to develop a range of consumer products, particularly in the field of textiles and food, which will be both attractive and marketable, and call upon a range of scientific and design knowledge. Many other institutions have similar initiatives, although overall the evidence is that we are not producing amongst us anything like the numbers of students skilled and educated to the standards industry is demanding.

Perhaps the most difficult question which faces us in the development of the curriculum in schools or in higher education, is the training of the existing and future teachers who will be needed to make such a curriculum live in ways which grasp and hold the enthusiasm of young people. Very few teachers in the present teaching population have the range of skills which are needed on their own, and the way ahead for them must be to work together in teams, combining those who have the intellectual mastery of science and mathematics to work with those who have the practical and applied skills in CDT, computing, home economics and art. Such an approach would have the added bonus of demonstrating to pupils the team work and co-operation which is a part of the message of how creative technology and design can be evolved in working life.

For the initial training phase, we must surely look both to this team approach amongst the teacher trainers, and draw more and more on the skills of those who work in the forefront of developing industries to contribute to the life of the schools, and to the knowledge and understanding of teachers. Perhaps we should be searching out ways to persuade those with such industrial and commercial experience to spend a part of their time teaching young people directly, whether on a part-time basis, on short secondment or even on temporary transfers into the teaching profession. They bring not only the fresh air of reality and commercial understanding into the school, but also the living examples of successful careers in fields where the pupils should be aspiring to follow.

Such success can only build on the right relationships between education and business. Inherent in everything to which we aspire, and in the education system's response to the challenge of technology, is the need for true partnerships between business and education: between teachers and other workers in the economy. Just as each depends upon the other for their life blood – teachers' pay comes from the taxes of private industry and commerce, while the enterprises rely on the products of the school to keep their workforce appropriately replenished – so as a society we cannot hope to respond adequately and quickly enough to the challenges of our changing world unless we work together in partnership.

The partnership implies the coming together of equals, and the most successful examples of education/business partnerships come from those where each side has recognised their need to understand and learn from the other, while developing an increasing understanding of the contribution each can make. While enterprises may provide the examples of technology use and technology application which our pupils and teachers need to experience, they can also supply direct teaching themselves in the school phase as well as in higher education. An extension of partnership in teaching company schemes, in sandwich placements and in industrially sponsored research students is widely recognised as an appropriate way ahead, and should remain a priority even in periods of industrial hardship as well as in times of economic prosperity. Economic recession provides a window of opportunity for schools to recruit experienced technologists and technicians from industry into the teaching profession, to contribute their experience to the classroom. By working together and learning each other's language and approach, people from education and business can enlarge their own experience, and enhance their own performance, in ways which provide us with a more integrated and sane society.

Some of the background papers for the colloquium provide examples of the range of possibilities open to educators in the use of the new technologies in our teaching and learning approaches. This is an area which will be increasingly important as the demands of the curriculum expand, and the expansion of higher education puts ever-increasing demands for sophisticated student learning approaches on our universities and colleges. One of the most powerful messages to young people about the applications of technology can be given implicitly in the way in which their schools, colleges and universities use the technologies as everyday tools in their learning experience.

The challenge is vast: at the present we still deny to far too many young people, most particularly to girls and women, the opportunity to participate fully as citizens in a technologically defined world. Business and education in partnership can offer access to the full privileges of citizenship in our technological society which is the birthright of every child and every adult in the community. This book explores some of the ways in which this challenge can be met.

The colloquium was generously supported by the Fulbright Commission, whose mission for the promotion of Anglo-American understanding is close to our hearts at South Bank. Thanks are also due to our colleagues and friends at City College, New York, without whose contribution the colloquium would not have been possible, and whose friendship and collaboration is valued in many spheres of this polytechnic's activity.

2

Policies for the future in the UK

SIR JOHN CAINES, KCB

In the past, the United States was regarded as the world leader in technological advance, and where the US leads, the UK sooner or later usually followed. However, the UK now has the will and the policies which will help to narrow the gap and even take the lead. It is particularly apt to link the twin themes of technology and education. Technology continually forces the pace of the educator while at the same time providing the means to help the educator to keep pace. Teachers cannot equip the youth of today to prepare for the future unless the teachers of today are equipped with today's technology.

The foundations needed for education to respond to the challenge of technology are already being laid. We have begun to give the UK the chance to equip itself for the twenty-first century. What is needed now is not further change but commitment to implement and see through the changes. This is a task for every teacher, for every local education authority and – one way or another – for every member of the Department of Education and Science. But it is also a task for every young person to grasp the new opportunities available. Every *individual* needs to appreciate the responsibility resting on him or her to chart a personal career, to get equipped with the skills, knowledge and qualifications needed for success wherever that success is sought.

It is a task in which the energies and commitment of *employers* need to be engaged too. If employers do not take enough interest in the education system they are not entitled to blame that system for failing to deliver the sort of human assets they will need. Traditionally, businessmen know about attending to the suppliers of goods and materials. They have grown to be even more attentive to the suppliers of capital. They are now being enjoined to involve themselves with the suppliers of the third and most precious factor of production – people. This factor more than any other will determine whether the UK succeeds or fails against international competition in the twenty-first century and whether it continues up the ladder of development – holding its own against the most developed nations of the world – or struggling to retain a foothold as the former developing countries of the world storm up the ladder and overtake the UK.

What sort of people does the UK need for success in the twenty-first century? Is it the same sort of person we prided ourselves on producing in the nineteenth century when many of the most deeply entrenched views about the role and content of education were established? Is it the same sort of person whom we tried to create in the twentieth century when we tinkered at the edges of the nineteenth-century model and still under-estimated the needs of our nation for ever-larger numbers of people with high levels of skill and qualifications? The twentieth century has been a time when we either exhausted ourselves in wars or believed that the things we were good at would endure forever only to find that others had been swifter to identify new market needs and swifter to adapt to the challenge they brought.

To value technological literacy as equal to academic ability is not to undervalue scholarship. Both capabilities are needed and worthy of the same concern. It is doubtful that the UK can succeed economically by relying on the production of brilliant inventions whilst neglecting the skills and knowledge needed to turn those inventions into sources of wealth creation.

The twentieth century has seen science and technology move to the centre stage and demonstrate a pace of development which leaves us gasping. I suspect that the twenty-first century will witness the same vertiginous pace and perhaps an even more hectic one. Those to whom we look to keep Britain in the twenty-first century advancing up the ladder and providing an ever-better quality of life for its inhabitants will need four characteristics:

Firstly, intellectual attainment: this is still the driving force behind progress and change. The higher education industry is not going to be put out of business. On the contrary, the demand for graduates will continue to grow even if the nature of those graduates may need to adapt and spread across more disciplines. Secondly, we shall need people who are technologically literate. I mean by this people who are able to make use of technology when they want to and in particular when the needs of the economy signal that they should do so. But these people also need to understand the effect that technology has on their daily lives, the scope that it gives to enrich those lives and the dangers if technology becomes the master and not the slave. It is an issue of attitudes as well as knowledge.

Thirdly, we shall need adaptability. Depth of knowledge will continue, of course, to be required. But those who are going to operate in the wealth-creating parts of our economy will need a greater variety of skills and attainments and the enterprise to put them to good use. Has over-specialisation in both education and training been putting a costly brake on our ability to adapt speedily to changing economic circumstances?

And there is a fourth feature which permeates all three: rechargeability. By this I mean the recognition that with rapidly changing technology the shelf life of knowledge and special skills gets shorter and shorter. Education will not cease at 16, it will not cease at 19, nor will it cease at 21, it will continue throughout life.

All four of those characteristics are crucial for the education system – the way it works and what it delivers through all its phases. In most of what follows the emphasis will be on the second of these – technological literacy.

Let me begin with the compulsory school years of 5–16 and, in particular, the National Curriculum. The National Curriculum is a response to concerns that schools have been failing to develop the full potential of all pupils – a response to concerns that in some important senses standards are not satisfactory. It is designed to lift standards by establishing clear, challenging and widely agreed objectives and a framework of content for each subject and by giving teachers and parents the means of checking how well those objectives are being met. In addition, it aims to give pupils a balanced education avoiding premature specialisation.

There are four basic elements of the National Curriculum and these are laid down in statute. The first is the list of subjects and there are ten 'main' or foundation subjects of which science is one and technology is another. Secondly, for each of these ten subjects, there are specified standards of knowledge, skill and understanding which pupils should attain as they progress through school: 'attainment targets'. For each attainment target there are precise definitions at ten levels of what pupils should know, be able to do and understand. These levels cover the full range of pupils' abilities during compulsory education. Thirdly, there are the programmes of study: the things pupils must learn and do in order to meet the attainment targets. Finally, there are the arrangements for identifying at four key stages, i.e. 7, 11, 14 and 16 years, how pupils are doing. This national assessment system provides information for teachers and parents about how their children are doing but also gives governing bodies, local authorities and the community at large a performance indicator about their schools.

What is National Curriculum technology? Indeed, what is meant by the very term, 'technology'? It has been stated: 'technology – the knack of so arranging the world that we don't have to experience it'; but technology is not about avoiding experience of the world. It is quite the reverse. It may indeed be easier to continue in this vein, saying what technology is not. It is not simply science, nor is it just applied science – though of course there are scientific applications within technology, and much of technology will build on scientific knowledge and understanding. Technology is not heavy engineering, nor is it craft, design and technology – CDT as we knew it and it is not just computers. It is a new and essentially *practical* subject which draws together, through a common approach, aspects of art and design, business studies, the old CDT, information technology and home economics – things which have individually been well established in British schools and colleges for some time but which have not before been brought together into a coherent discipline for all pupils to study.

This common approach embraces identifying needs and opportunities, designing, planning and making and evaluating. It is this approach which underlies the technology curriculum and needs to be applied to a broad range of materials – wood, metal, plastic, textiles and food, to name but a few – to plan, design, produce and evaluate a range of products – systems and environments as well as artifacts. And in the course of this approach, pupils will also have to take account of issues such as safety, cost and aesthetic considerations, and whether their ideas would benefit or harm the environment. Information technology is present in the technology curriculum in two forms. Firstly, it has an attainment target of its own, thus guaranteeing that all children will learn to use it. Secondly, it features extensively in other parts of the technology curriculum and is present in some form in virtually all parts of the National Curriculum.

What happens when our scientifically sensitised and technologically acute pupils reach the age of 16? They may stay on at school or decide to go to a sixth form or further education college, maybe with a view to entering higher education at 18. They may go straight into employment. For those who go on to A levels the preparation provided by the National Curriculum could well result in more students of both sexes opting for science and technology and choosing for study at A level and at degree level those subjects which have a scientific or technological bias. But A-level students are not the only group to consider. We must also consider the needs of the 70 per cent of the school population who do not embark on A levels. Too many young people do not develop their potential to the full because they have not found an acceptable alternative to academic studies after the age of 16. This is an area where there is still much more to be done. As Kenneth Baker pointed out in an important speech in 1989 when he was Secretary of State for Education, further education is of fundamental importance and has tended to be the Cinderella of the education service. Participation rates for 16- and 17-year olds in education or training (full-time or part-time) are not as bad as many would have us believe. The most recent international comparison relates to 1986 and showed the UK at 75 per cent (similar to France and Australia) but admittedly lower than Germany's 96 per cent. By 1989 that UK figure had climbed to 85 per cent.

The traditional role of further education (FE) colleges has been to provide technological education in support of industrial and commercial training. Some colleges of further education reflect this tradition in their names: 'technical colleges' or 'colleges of technology'. Some trace their roots back to the nineteenth century reflecting an earlier effort to provide a technical curriculum to complement the predominantly academic tradition of schools. The FE colleges' response to the needs of industry includes not just off-the-job training for apprentices but also an indispensable service to employers for the retraining of adults in various aspects of technology.

Kenneth Baker called for action on three fronts. One of those fronts was action on the image and marketing of further education and things are in hand to bring that about. The new Further Education Marketing Unit commenced work in 1990. The unit's objectives are to project a fresh, positive image of further education to employers and young people and to raise their awareness of the facilities on offer. It also provides a consultancy service to colleges and LEAs on marketing, media relations and promotions.

Two other strands are also being translated into action. Under the 1988 Education Reform Act, FE colleges have become more independent with greater power over their own finances, staffing and courses. The freedoms they have won will enable them to be more responsive and more entrepreneurial.

The third strand relates to qualifications and the curriculum. There are four levels of award, many of them in fields of technology, established by the National Council for Vocational Qualifications, leading to higher education. The aim is to provide opportunities in the vocational field to match those in the academic. A levels, together with AS levels, will of course continue to represent the gold standard for rigour and academic achievement but they are not the only route. Vocational courses can and do provide an alternative path to higher skills and higher education. Those courses are valid in their own right and pursuing them has no stigma.

There are no plans to extend the pre–16 National Curriculum to the post–16 student but the DES does encourage ideas about core skills, ideas about modularisation and credit transfer. Students who have been tempted to pursue academic routes unsuited to their talents need to be able to move without loss of face or attainment to other routes. Students who have not aspired to higher education need to be able to demonstrate whether they have the potential to succeed in higher education. In all of this there is much to learn from the example of the USA.

In higher education (HE) we move, of course, into very different territory. The institutions delivering higher education are independent and attendance at them is entirely voluntary. The government does not seek to prescribe standards or establish the curriculum. Its role is to determine the framework within which the institutions go about their business and to provide such funds as it thinks fit to sustain and assist that business, having regard to the benefits which the community at large derives from the availability of higher education. The basic aims of government policy are to encourage greater participation in higher education, to promote an efficient and market-oriented higher-education sector, and to strengthen the independence of the sector by encouraging diversification of funding. These aims are highly relevant to the needs of the twenty-first century. These aims are being achieved. There are now over one million students. Ten years ago one in eight young people entered HE; in 1991, one in five. By the end of the decade the figure will be one in four.

Higher education is too often seen as full-time provision for young people studying for their first degree. This is the most significant client group, but there are others – not least the increasing number of those returning to higher education for up-dating courses of various lengths. All these needs are met through a mix of full-time, sandwich and part-time courses. The interaction between institutions, students and employers means that the curricula of these courses are changing to reflect industry's needs to recruit and retrain. It is encouraging to see how higher education institutions are now willing to search out and develop potential talent which might otherwise have remained dormant. There is a big market there to be tapped. Eighty per cent of the workforce of the year 2000 is already at work. Much of it is not equipped with the skills and knowledge needed for a technological age. Many of those who have some technological skills and knowledge are equipped with outdated versions.

The polytechnic sector has responded particularly well in the drive to widen access to higher education without any loss in the quality of output. Overall enrolments have increased by more than 40 per cent in the last ten years. Part-time students are a strong feature – the sector accounts for the great majority of such enrolments outside the Open University. A commitment to widening access and equal opportunities is a commonly stated feature of polytechnics' strategic plans. Target groups include mature students, women, ethnic minorities, the unemployed, and students with non-standard entry qualifications. Several polytechnics now have 20 to 30 per cent of their enrolments from non-traditional entry students.

Widening access further will depend on institutions' ability to continue to demonstrate that they are offering bankable skills to their prospective students. This is especially true in the case of mature students. They are not going to sacrifice earnings in the short term, or give up their leisure, in order to return to or take up study if the qualification they obtain at the end of the day has no currency with employers. Similarly, young people will increasingly want to be confident that the skills they acquire by enrolling on a higher education course are in demand. I suggest that successful expansion of higher education in the 1990s and beyond will mean further cementing the alliance between academic values and methods and their application in the practical world: relevance, in short.

One of the best means of ensuring relevance lies in the further development of higher education institutions' already burgeoning links with business: applied research undertaken on behalf of business customers; consultancies provided by academic staff; PICKUP (Professional, Industrial and Commercial Updating) and short-course provision; secondment of staff to industry and commerce.

The Department of Employment's Enterprise in Higher Education Programme enables higher education to help students handle the real economy more effectively. It assists higher education institutions to develop enterprising graduates in partnership with employers. In recent years, departments in individual universities, polytechnics and colleges have sought to embed the concept and practice of enterprise in higher education. The Enterprise in Higher Education Programme enables higher education institutions to consolidate these efforts and build on them. Participating institutions receive financial support provided that they can also secure support, in cash or in kind, from employers in their localities. Since the programme started in 1988, over forty institutions have been selected to participate: a further group of institutions was added in 1992.

Let us now consider information technology (IT) in education. The UK leads the world – even the USA – in IT in schools. This position has been achieved by wise investment. The introduction of IT took place when little was known about its potential application in education. Two complementary pilot programmes were a considerable success – the Department of Trade and Industry's micros in schools scheme, which helped to provide the hardware, and the DES Microelectronics Education Programme which stimulated action on software production and teacher training and set up an information network.

Building on that success LEAs took over the lead, and a microelectronics education support unit, later the National Council for Educational Technology, was established to support them. The DES then, on behalf of the taxpayer, invested heavily, with a £75 million programme over the three years up to March 1991 and through specific grants to support LEA activity. There has also been substantial investment from industry into particular schools in their areas. This initiative provides a model for successful collaboration between central government, local government and industry. On average there are 4.3 micros for each primary school (2.5 in 1988) and forty-one machines for each secondary school (twenty-three in 1988).

Without so many micros in schools with teachers trained to use them, it would not have been possible to contemplate a National Curriculum into which IT had been built so extensively. Besides the separate attainment target for IT in technology, there is also a separate attainment target in science on the scientific aspects of IT. In other subjects – English, maths, geography, modern foreign languages – there will be recognition of the use and function of IT. Building on this, the Secretary of State has accepted, in principle, the National Curriculum Council's recommendation that IT should be one of the core skills for all students aged 16–19.

Within further education, IT is firmly embedded in many courses. For example, in engineering workshops, the rows of milling machines and capstan lathes are being replaced by computer-numerically controlled and computer-aided design equipment; in college hairdressing salons, students maintain computer-based customer records; and on other courses students learn how to operate effectively within the electronic office. In the arts and humanities, IT assists in the learning of languages and English. IT also provides another example of the FE colleges' responsiveness to the needs of industry. Many colleges have produced courses tailor-made for companies, and these tend to focus particularly on IT.

In higher education too, the influence of IT is all-pervasive. The government has taken an active role in stimulating the use of IT in higher education and research through the creation and funding of the Computer Board. This has worked hard to bring a real coherence to academic and research computing both within and between institutions. The open Joint Academic Network (JANET) is the envy of many countries. IT links the UK's major higher education institutions and research centres as well as board-funded national computing centres which provide the latest computing technology and data sets beyond the reach of individual institutions. The joint 'computers in teaching initiative' was established by the Computer Board and the then University Grants Committee with the purpose of getting the use of IT firmly bedded into the wider curriculum.

Much of the initiative has come from institutions themselves. But the fruits of all this are startling. For example, in engineering, the single most important technical influence on the curriculum has been the growth of IT. IT has now become a field of study in its own right. Here polytechnics and colleges have been responding to the large and growing demand for qualified people with high levels of IT and computing skills. They have developed a range of IT and computing courses at diploma, first degree, post-experience and post-graduate levels to meet the needs of students and potential or existing employers. These courses have been very successful: nine out of ten of those graduating from polytechnic first degree courses in computer science in 1988 obtained permanent employment in the UK within six months of graduating – compared with an average of two-thirds.

In higher education, as elsewhere, IT is also an essential enabling technology in many other disciplines. For example, business and management departments are mostly attempting to use IT both as a business tool and as an aid to teaching and learning. In civil engineering, building, surveying and planning courses, IT is well integrated in the curriculum, and there has been a considerable investment in computing facilities in recent years. Overall, there has been a dramatic increase in both the number and variety of specific computer applications which give students an introduction to, and experience of, computers in their field of study. And even where that does not happen, in many cases students are given a general computer appreciation or IT literacy course.

In all phases of education technology is not just a challenge for the content of learning. It is proving to be an agent for improving the quality and efficiency of teaching and learning. It facilitates more individual study and can help pupils and students to learn by themselves and give them greater autonomy in the way they study. IT is therefore also a catalyst for change in the role of the teacher. The teacher is no longer the sole means of delivering information and expertise to children. But here I feel I must sound a note of caution: let no one think that teachers are replaceable by computers. As Walter Lippman said as long ago as 1914: 'you cannot endow even the best machine with initiative; the jolliest steamroller will not plant flowers'. The same sentiment was expressed rather more succinctly, though in rather less picturesque a fashion, by John F. Kennedy in 1963: 'man is the most extraordinary computer of all'. There is no replacement for teachers of quality in schools and colleges. IT will increasingly release teachers from the time consuming task of giving out information so that they can concentrate on the great skill of teaching children *how* to learn.

But if IT opens up this potential, it is essential that teachers are equipped to fulfil their role, through their initial teacher training, through in-service training, and through simple contact with the world of business. The government is taking steps to ensure that all new teachers have the basic skills required to use IT effectively in the classroom. All training courses now contain compulsory and clearly identifiable elements in IT for every student. All students are now expected to emerge from their training with certain specified, practical competencies in the use of IT for their teaching. They must, for example, be able to judge how useful a range of software will be for teaching a particular subject and age range and then be able to use it appropriately in their lessons.

CONCLUSION

In conclusion, I have been seeking to demonstrate that the UK is putting into place the policies that will enable all pupils and students to become technologically literate and thus to meet at least some of the challenges of the twenty-first century. I think it important to suggest that perhaps technology does not always provide all the answers. Technology may help us along the road, but it does not tell us where we should be going in the first place. Put another way, as Charles M. Allen said in 1967: 'if the human race wants to go to hell in a basket, technology can help it to get there by jet. It won't change the desire or the direction, but it can greatly speed the passage'. Our current emphasis on technology does not mean that there is no longer a place for the traditional academic subjects; indeed technology can facilitate their study. But technological and academic subjects should have equality of status. As the National Curriculum Council stated in its November 1989 report to the Secretary of State: 'technology is the one subject in the National Curriculum that is directly concerned with generating ideas, making and doing. In emphasising the importance of practical capability and providing opportunities for pupils to develop their powers to innovate, to make decisions, to create new solutions, it can play a unique role. Central to this role is the task of providing balance in a curriculum based on academic subjects'.

This has not been the only theme in this chapter. The other has been that of partnership and relevance. There are challenges to both education institutions and employers. Educational institutions cannot afford to take clients for granted – they may find that they no longer have any. In fact, educational institutions are well placed to respond to expressed needs and demands, and have consistently demonstrated their ability to do so. In their turn, industry and employers should not expect the education system intuitively to know what is required of it, and should not expect it to succeed without their help. The challenges of the technological twenty-first century will be immense. If we are to meet them in a way which, as a nation, we barely managed to do *this* century, a mighty effort will be needed. *This* time we cannot afford the luxury of an untrained workforce nor of a remote academic intelligentsia. *This* time there can be no spectators of the technological revolution. We must all play our part and we must play to win.

3

Teachers' and schools' response to the challenge

SIR WILLIAM TAYLOR

'Technology' in relation to education can be approached from a great variety of angles. The *Concise Oxford* defines it, intriguingly, as 'the science of the industrial arts'. But in much contemporary usage, it is the *metaphorical* character of 'technology' that is to the fore. The term has entered our discourse as a descriptor for societies and economies that are increasingly dependent on the use of mechanical and electronic means of transportation, production, communication, distribution and exchange. The cultural, social and psychological consequences for societies and economies so organised permeate every aspect of the lives of states and of citizens, not least their political and educational arrangements.

In most discussions about technology in education, however, the current focus of interest is much narrower and programmatic. The emphasis is on changing the attitudes, values and practices of teachers and schools in ways that will strengthen the competitive advantage and economic well-being of the United Kingdom, or Europe, the increasingly irrelevantly labelled 'Western world', or some other common interest group.

Most conferences and meetings in this field try to get a handle on how educational policies, administrative arrangements, curriculum content, teaching methods, and that network of connections that makes up the interface between formal education and subsequent employment can enthuse, motivate and empower men and women to act in ways that encourage innovation, enhance productivity, ensure economic success, develop human potential and (increasingly popular themes) help developing countries and protect the environment.

There appear to be two dominant sets of responses to such an agenda. One is to deny its assumptions and challenge its objectives. Another, much more commonly adopted, is to select a small number of manageable activities and to consider in detail how these might be initiated, put in place and evaluated. Among the latter I would include the setting up of school/industry 'compacts', the attempt to develop attitudes and practices among teachers conducive to 'enterprise values', and, in the case of higher education institutions, the creation of specialised agencies to facilitate technology transfer and industrial innovation.

Neither category of response – outright rejection of all that the machine means for education and for society on the one hand, the detailed discussion of means and methods on the other – tackles the principal challenges that educators confront in relation to the ubiquitous technology in all its aspects. In this chapter I aim to establish the particular character of that challenge.

THE ROOTS OF REJECTION

A leading industrialist said recently that if the Universities were to contribute adequately to the economic life of the country, they needed essentially to produce enough men who said 'Yes' to the industrial process. Yet, by and large, the teaching profession consists of those who have said 'No' to it.

(Peterson 1968)

This 'no-saying' on the part of many has been a cause of concern for governments in both the United Kingdom and the United States. Its roots are both deep and (to succumb to a currently over-used expression) non-trivial. They have been explored by a succession of historians and cultural analysts. In the British case, it is argued that traditional mercantile and agrarian values, unbroken by revolutions of the kind that convulsed other countries, successfully resisted emergent industrial values and continued to dominate educational provision. Similarly, the great developments in academic science in the second half of the nineteenth century placed a high value on disciplinary specialisation, contrary to the earlier premium on synthesis. The scientist, a title to which students of history, of education and of many other emerging disciplines aspired, achieved status not by proposing new syntheses or identifying practical applications in such fields as engineering, but by making a contribution to advancing a specialism.

Another factor encouraging anti-industrial and anti-technological values was the impact on public consciousness of the deplorable social conditions of nineteenth- and early twentieth-century industrial Britain. These conditions were railed against from many directions. One source was the arts and crafts movement, in which Ruskin, Morris and other anti-bourgeois, romantically inspired interpreters played an important part. Thoughtful churchmen saw and spoke out against the moral debasement that industrialisation entailed, not only for its victims, but also for those who profited from its successes. Socialist reformers were less concerned about cultural debasement and philistinism than lack of educational opportunity and occupational mobility. None of these groups showed much interest in the problems of production and the threat of international competition to which writers such as Thomas Huxley had drawn attention in the mid nineteenth century (Taylor 1985).

There are still plenty of educators today who share the values of the influential typographer and sculptor Eric Gill, who in the early years of this century preached 'the forgotten truth that industrially based capitalism is *untrue* to the nature of man' (McCarthy 1989). There is a contemporary vein of neo-marxist, post-modernist, and ecologically aware writing which argues for the outright rejection of values seen to be irredeemably associated with industrial and technological success. Here is a recent brief and pointed formulation:

> Allowing ends to be defined by a technological process which publishes no statement of its intention, *all* regimes which are oriented by a technological sensibility separate means from ends and become pre-occupied with the refinement and amplification of the means. Thus counterveiling as well as dominant regimes are implicated in a process in which means absorb ends until, it so happens, the means become ends. Instrumentalism, it is easy to conclude, becomes its own excuse for being; duly ontologised, becomes true being.
>
> (Kariels 1990).

Some teachers tend, not because of the imposition of some progressive child-centred ideology, but because of the way in which their role overlaps that of the parent and the family, to value individual performance and achievement in its own terms, rather than comparatively and competitively. They deprecate those external constraints that appear to thwart the full development of human potential, those walls of necessity and contingency that inhibit the full, individual flowering of the human spirit in whatever form it manifests itself in the single pupil.

Such a position is neither sentimental nor naive. It has its roots in some of the greatest traditions of our civilisation, in the respect for the individual on which much of our law and social practice is based. We can respect and value such an individualistic focus. We cannot and should not ignore its possible consequences. There might have been a time when individualism, pastoralism, a yearning for a return to simpler, community-based sources of satisfaction, was a viable option not just for cults and for minorities, but for whole populations. If ever that option existed, it does not exist today. There are simply too many of us.

We reject (but are not always able to avoid) the depredations of the four horsemen of the apocalypse – famine, pestilence, war and death. But if the hungry are to be fed and new demands on the economy and the environment contained, it must be by means of technology – intermediate, appropriate or whatever its name, but technology just the same. Global interdependence based upon growing, fattening, making and selling is now so great that, save for small privileged minorities, 'contracting out' becomes impossible. Teachers, schools and universities are part of a process now so pervasive that its outright rejection is no longer an option.

COMING TO TERMS WITH TECHNOLOGY

What from all this can we identify as the central role of teachers in schools in relation to technology? Let us learn from our critics, and keep technology in perspective as a means rather than an end. How by such a means do we ensure that a high and increasing proportion of the world's peoples are fed, clothed, and provided with satisfying work? How can technology help people to live securely within culturally diverse communities, be made happy and educated in ways that maximise human potential? How can it assist in offering the protection of just laws, and minimise damage to the lives of other individuals and groups or to the natural environment? How can technology enable society to meet the needs and expectations of its people in ways that facilitate effective and rule-bound governance and civic order?

Failure in the international marketplace is not conducive to such ends. Hence the importance that governments of all colours attach to the role of teachers and schools in enhancing market success. In his recent and widely quoted book *The Competitive Advantage of Nations*, Michael Porter (1990) identifies education as a significant aspect of the 'factor creation' which makes for such success. His analysis of the position in the United States and in the United Kingdom is unflattering. It coincides with that of numerous official and unofficial commissions and committees of the 1980s, identifying: lack of investment in human resources; low standards other than at the top of the educational hierarchy; weak discipline; inadequate training. All this has become so familiar, on both sides of the Atlantic, that it is now tending to wash over the heads of teachers and administrators who feel themselves under equipped to meet the weight of criticism piled upon them.

Since the beginning of the 1980s, there has been no lack of effort in this country or, as I understand it, in the United States, to remedy deficiences of the kind identified by Porter. It is easy to argue, as some critics of teachers, schools and universities have done, that the system which most of the contributors to this book have helped to create and sustain are proving impervious or resistant to ideas and innovations essential for maintaining and enhancing competitive advantage and economic success. But it has to be remembered that whilst schools and teachers were once the chief, if not for many children the only, providers of knowledge, information, attitudes and values, today this is no longer the case.

The six hours or so spent in school each day between the ages of 5 and 18 may still be the most systematically organised sources of knowledge and attitude formation, but the other ten waking hours are permeated with an enormous volume of words and images which selectively reinforce or counter the messages of formal education and training. Furthermore, the concept of 'standards' which has achieved iconic status, needs to be unpacked before we can begin comparing past and present.

TECHNOLOGY AND CURRICULUM

During the 1980s there was a number of official and non-official UK initiatives to relate technology more directly to the work of teachers and schools – such as the Confederation of British Industry's 'Understanding British Industry' (UBI) project, or the Governments' Technical Vocational Education Initiative (TVEI). These retain importance. These are discussed elsewhere. The focus of attention here should be upon those elements of the new National Curriculum which seek to enhance economic and industrial understanding and to provide appropriate careers education and guidance.

The National Curriculum comprises three core subjects (mathematics, English and science, with Welsh in those schools where it is the medium of instruction) and seven other foundation subjects (history, geography, technology, music, art, PE and modern foreign language). The knowledge, skills and understanding which pupils of different abilities are expected to have achieved in each subject area are specified in terms of up to ten levels of attainment within each of the four key stages at or near the end of which national assessment takes place. Specialist groups have been set up to advise on curriculum appropriate to each attainment target. These groups issue interim reports on a consultative basis, to which the Secretary of State responds. The groups final report is then used as the basis for the Statutory Orders issued by government in respect of each foundation subject.

In addition, the National Curriculum Council (NCC) has defined a number of cross-curricular elements in terms of dimensions, skills and themes. Dimensions are meant to permeate every aspect of the curriculum. They include such matters as the provision of equal opportunities. Skills include those of communication, numeracy, study, problem solving, personal and social and information technology which the NCC 'considers it absolutely essential . . . are fostered across the whole curriculum in a measured and planned way' (NCC 1990).

Finally, there are five themes: economic and industrial understanding, careers education and guidance, health education, education for citizenship, and environmental education. Clearly, these are overlapping, but the focus of our current concern is upon the first two – economic and industrial understanding, and careers education and guidance. The council's summary statement of the first of these is worth quoting in full:

> Education for economic and industrial understanding aims to help pupils make decisions such as how to organise their finances and how to spend their money. It involves controversial issues such as government economic policy in the impact of economic activity on the environment. It prepares pupils for their future economic role as producers, consumers and citizens in a democracy. Pupils need to understand enterprise and wealth creation and to develop entrepreneurial skills.
>
> Education for economic and industrial understanding should cover aspects of industry and the economy such as business, commerce, finance and consumer affairs. Pupils should have direct experience of industry and the world of work and take part in small scale business and community enterprise projects.

It has been recognised that there is little point in teaching children of primary and secondary school age about technology unless at the same time they understand the elementary economic principles that determine which technological possibilities will or will not be exploited and marketed. The NCC has published guidance on how aspects of economic and industrial understanding can be fostered through each of the foundation subjects of the curriculum (Table 3.1).

Table 3.1 Education for economic and industrial understanding

Foundation subjects	Economic and industrial understanding	
Mathematics	Calculating personal monies	Money management (income, expenditure and savings)
	Statistical analysis of food prices	Price and the cost of living
Science	Recycling and disposal of waste	Scarcity, needs and wants
	Studying energy production, e.g. a petroleum refinery	Economic resources and production
English	Talking about different types of work	Employment and the division of labour
	Reading literature concerning poverty	Distribution of wealth
Technology	Applying technological innovations to production	Efficiency and productivity
	Enterprise activity, involving a business plan forecasting cash flows	Investment, risk and marketing, supply and demand
History	Long-distance trade routes in the sixteenth century	Supply and demand, and foreign trade
	Handloom weavers and factories	Scales of production
Geography	Provision of goods and services in the local economy	Producers and consumers
	Impact of planning decisions on the environment	Costs and benefits
Modern foreign languages	Foreign visits and tourism	Foreign money and exchange rates
	Understanding the importance of foreign languages for business	Marketing, imports and exports, and the balance of payments

Source: NCC 1990a; 1990b.

In addition to what is done within the formal curriculum, there is an enormous variety of activity now being undertaken by schools involving, for example, work observation and site visits; careers guidance presentations; work experience and work shadowing; mini enterprise activities, in which groups of children operate 'businesses'; and 'compacts', originating in Boston and now increasingly a feature of business-school relations in English cities.

The hope must be that the knowledge and understanding achieved by these means will make for more positive attitudes towards making and selling, will encourage values of enterprise and entrepreneural behaviour, and motivate young people, through developing their own potential, to make active and effective contributions to the economic, social and personal well-being of their fellows.

Given that conscious efforts to achieve these ends through the curriculum and in other school activities have being going on only since the mid 1970s, it is too early to say whether in the UK, or in other countries, teachers and schools can adapt to new ways of thinking, counteract the powerlessness, meaninglessness, isolation and self-estrangement that can be generated by negative work experience, and endow young people with the literacy, numeracy and social competence that will enable them to adapt to personal and communal circumstances as yet unenvisaged.

THE NEED FOR A STRATEGY

What is already clear at every level is that links between schools and universities and business will not succeed unless they are part of a clear strategy. In higher education some of the more common failings have arisen because schemes have been implemented too quickly for proper consideration to be given to priorities and opportunity costs. Many links have been ad hoc. Personal contact between individual academics and industrialists can be a good way of getting things going, but without appropriate co-ordination, energies and efforts soon dissipate.

Another weakness is a failure to recognise that the interests of the individual academic, the department and the institution are not always easily reconciled. Financial exigency and media interest emphasise total project cost at the expense of proper infrastructure and adequate margins. Institutions can find that 'million dollar deals' arranged by individual academics constitute a string of unplanned loss makers and onerous benefactions. A focus on add-on and one-off research consultancy and post-experience training, valuable as they are, can divert attention from the importance to business of the process and output of mainstream teaching. On occasion, playing down differences in the ideologies, priorities and values of academic and industrial institutions, better to stimulate short run collaboration, has generated unrealistic expectations and disappointing outcomes.

Nor is it always the case that sufficient attention is given to ensuring that mechanisms and procedures set up to encourage and facilitate collaboration with business – liaison officers, costing and pricing arrangements, research consortia – are understood and utilised by those whose work they are intended to facilitate within and beyond the institutions. Such topics will be addressed elsewhere in this volume. It is sufficient to say that weaknesses of this kind are not restricted to higher education institutions; they can diminish the effectiveness of effort at every level, not least in primary and secondary schools.

PREPARING THE TEACHER

Given that the proportion of the teaching force made up of the newly qualified is small, most of the training necessary to ensure that teachers can organise their programmes and assessment in accordance with the new requirements must inevitably be in-service. Over the past years, schools and local authorities have organised courses, conferences and events to ensure that teachers are equipped for their new task. Pilot studies of assessment at key stage one have been undertaken, in the light of which a number of modifications have been made to the methods of assessment to be employed, intended to simplify what was emerging as a formidable task of observing and recording behaviour.

As far as initial training is concerned, a number of statements in the criteria promulgated by the Secretary of State, which every recognised course of initial teacher training must now satisfy, (DES 1989) include references to economic and industrial understanding. For example, the following sections state:

'This element in courses should develop in students competence in key professional skills. It should also enable students to appreciate their task as teachers within the broad framework of the purposes of education, the development and structure of the education service, the values and the economic and other foundations of the free and civilised society in which their pupils are growing up, and the need to prepare pupils for adulthood, citizenship and the world of work.

6.2 On completion of their course, students should be aware of the links and common ground between subjects and be able to incorporate in their teaching cross-curricular dimensions (e.g. equal opportunities, multicultural education and personal and social education), themes (e.g. environmental education, economic and industrial understanding, health education and the European Dimension in education) and skills (e.g. oracy, literacy and numeracy).

6.7 Courses should also cover other aspects of the teacher's work, including:

iv   the significance of links between schools and the wider community; including those between schools, local businesses and the world of work;'

The Department of Trade and Industry (DTI) have funded a national project called 'Enterprise Awareness in Teacher Education' (EATE) designed to stimulate awareness on the part of teacher educators of their students' responsibilities in regard to appropriate themes within the National Curriculum.

Ways in which business and education have been co-operating at the primary and secondary stage that are relevant to professional formation include: personal contacts between heads, teachers and industrialists; participation in the activities of link organisations; twinning of schools with local companies; activities which involve both teachers and industrial members in common tasks, or simply for social purposes; the development of mini-companies; closer involvement of industrial representatives on the governing bodies of schools; the attendance of teachers at company or union meetings; the organisation of community projects jointly by schools and industry; exchange schemes whereby teachers work in industry or people from industry in schools for longer or shorter periods; practical help from industry for local schools in the form of technical advice and the use of specialist equipment; two-way visits and the provision of speakers; industrial tutor schemes; the employment of simulations, business games and problem-solving exercises; design-and-make competitions, and the joint development of industry-related materials for use in the curriculum and of in-service training.

Within initial teacher education institutions themselves there is an equally varied range of co-operative activity. Visits, placements, workshops, work shadowing, mini-enterprises, and many other initiatives currently feature in a rapidly developing range of activities.

Chris Marsden, manager of the Educational Relations Unit of British Petroleum, which has provided long-standing support for education-industry links, offers a useful analysis of the cross pressures to which both industry and schools are exposed. As Figure 3.1 (Marsden 1988) shows, both industry and schools have a 'bottom line', in the one case profit, in the other 'results'. In either field, however, to ignore the importance of the 'horizontal outputs' – the effects on the environment,

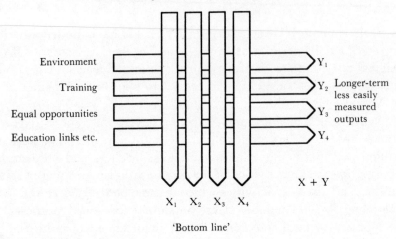

Business outputs matrix
A company's main products or services

Environment

Training

Equal opportunities

Education links etc.

Y_1

Y_2

Y_3

Y_4

Longer-term
less easily
measured
outputs

$X + Y$

X_1 X_2 X_3 X_4

'Bottom line'

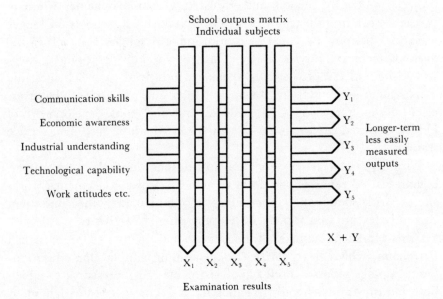

School outputs matrix
Individual subjects

Communication skills

Economic awareness

Industrial understanding

Technological capability

Work attitudes etc.

Y_1

Y_2

Y_3

Y_4

Y_5

Longer-term
less easily
measured
outputs

$X + Y$

X_1 X_2 X_3 X_4 X_5

Examination results

3.1 Business and school outputs matrices (Marsden 1988)

on quality of training, the provision of equal opportunities, and the generation of community and education links on the part of a business, and communication skills, economic awareness, industrial understanding, technological capability and work attitudes on the part of a school – is to weaken the long-term capacity to deliver a viable 'bottom line'.

In this connection, Marsden draws attention to a finding that has been as true in respect of primary and secondary education as at tertiary levels, namely the interest on the part of employers in the 'horizontal outputs'. The possession of appropriate skills of communication, understanding of industry, and the capacity to adapt to changing circumstances, can all be as valuable to the employer as the specific knowledge and skills to which the possession of formal credentials is testimony. For a high proportion of the workforce, subject knowledge is the means by which education takes place, rather than its end. We do not just study 'subjects'. We learn *through* subject study.

The Engineering Council and the Further Education Unit (1988) have promoted the idea of 'key technologies', which are likely to be important irrespective of the particular direction that technology takes in an unpredictable future:

> In preparing students for an uncertain future, educational institutions need to enable them to learn fundamental principles, including design, which underpin the development of specialist expertise as well as economic awareness and associated management and business skills.

Using a notion introduced by Bruner Figure 3.2 (Bruner 1960), they propose a model of the 'spiral curriculum' in which technology and economic awareness are closely allied.

CONCLUSION

The attempt to introduce explicitly industry- and technology-related materials and experiences into the primary and secondary curriculum has been criticised from two main directions. There are those who fear the consequences for the aspirations and achievements of working-class students of a new vocationalism, or who dislike the conservative 'correspondence' between curricular content and capitalism. Other critics perceive a threat to the importance and primacy of subject disciplines, a loss of emphasis on the basics of literacy and numeracy, and the possible neglect of literature and humanities. Both tendencies take the view that specific technology and industry-oriented skills and knowledge are best acquired post-school or by means of on-the-job training,

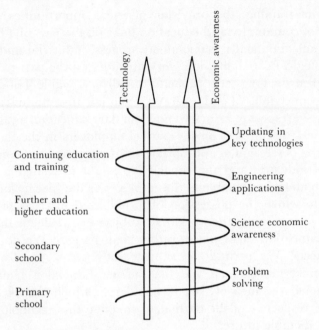

3.2 The 'spiral curriculum' (Bruner 1960)

and are more likely to take root in a well-worked tilth of disciplinary understanding than in the thinner soil of work experience and core skills.

I have some sympathy with these views. But I have a different interpretation of what constitutes the real challenge to schools and to teachers. It consists in devising a curriculum and range of experiences that successfully reconcile five related but not necessarily consistent purposes.

Firstly, high priority must be given to securing *for* every student access to the best that has been written, painted, sculpted, composed, and built in our own and other cultures, and to developing the full potential *of* every student for contributing to and building upon that heritage. This entails that the distinctive 'forms of knowledge' will continue to be a highly significant element in organising curricula at primary, secondary and tertiary levels.

Secondly, explicit attention will need to be given to the 'horizontal outputs' in Marsden's model, which include technology awareness and industrial and economic understanding. Some such outcomes can be secured, as the NCC argue, by an appropriate choice of content within the subject curriculum. Specific provision may still have to be made, however, to ensure an adequate focus on the types of experience to be offered, the knowledge to be acquired and the attitudes and behaviour to be fostered that will best develop appropriate understanding and skill.

Third, we must ensure that access to technological careers is opened up to larger numbers of women and members of minority groups. Positive action in this direction begins at the pre-school stage. It needs to continue throughout the primary and secondary school. In this rests one of the main hopes for overcoming the skill shortages that will otherwise weaken industrial competitiveness in the rest of the 1990s and the twenty-first century.

Fourthly, students need to be aware that technology is not autonomous, that there is nothing inevitable about the adoption of a particular *techne*, that both individually and collectively, men and women have choices to make. In the words of Winner (quoted Willoughby 1990: 321)

> If it is clear that the social contract implicitly created by implementing a particular generic variety of technology is incompatible with the kind of society we would deliberately choose, then that kind of device or system ought to be excluded from society altogether. A crucial failure of modern political theory has been its inability or unwillingness even to begin this project: critical evaluation of society's technical constitution. The silence of modern liberalism on this issue is matched by an equally obvious neglect in Marxist theory. Both persuasions have enthusiastically sought freedom in sheer material plenitude, welcoming whatever technological means (or monstrosities) seemed to produce abundance fastest.

This entails that political education must be fostered both through the disciplines and by means of specially devised experiences – and by teachers who do not themselves think in terms of populist cliches or whose environmental and ecological understanding is informed more by outrage than by information.

Fifthly, it will have to be recognised that in terms of the social and political changes with which students will need to contend in their future lives, technology is not the only nor necessarily the dominant influence. Appadurai (1990) posits the issue of disjunctures in the rates and direction of change between several dimensions of economic, political and social life. These include *ethnoscapes* – tourists, immigrants, refugees, exiles, guest workers and other persons and groups who move around the world; *mediascapes* – image-centred, narrative-based accounts of 'strips of reality'; *technoscapes* – the capacity of technology to move quickly across boundaries, not simply driven by market possibilities or economies or scale, but by complex relationships between politics, money flows and the availability of labour; *financescapes* – the disposition of global capital, and finally, *ideoscapes* – concatenations of images and ideas, many in our own case originating with the master narrative of the Enlightenment. In such a world, an education that is too narrowly technical will disable rather than empower.

This is a demanding agenda. It argues the need to do far more than foster technological awareness or provide marketable skills. Unless and until such awareness and skills are taught and learned within this broader framework, our students will be the slaves of technology, not its beneficiaries. As educators, it is our duty and responsibility to ensure that technology serves these larger purposes of expanding human potential, opening up opportunities and adding to the global sum of happiness and fulfilment. This book aims to make a significant contribution to our understanding of and commitment to the use and control of technology for the benefit of our students and our fellow men and women.

References

Appadurai A. (1990), 'Disjuncture and difference in the Global Economy'. In M. Featherstone (ed.), *Global Culture* London, Sage (*A Theory, Culture and Society* special issue).

Bruner J. S. (1960), *The Process of Education*, Cambridge, Mass., Harvard University Press.

Department of Education and Science (1989), *Initial Teacher Training: Approval of Courses* (Circular 24/89), London, Department of Education and Science.

Carlson C. G. (1990), *Beyond High School: the transition to work*, Focus 25, Princeton NJ, Educational Testing Service.

Cassels J. (1990), *Britain's Real Skill Shortage*, London, Policy Studies Institute.

Engineering Council and Further Education Unit (1988), *The Key Technologies*, London, EC and FEU.

Kariels H. S. (1990), 'The end game of post-modernism within the momentful of modernity', *Futures*, 22: 1.

Marsden C. (1988), *Why Business Should Work with Education*, London, British Petroleum.

McCarthy F. (1989), *Eric Gill*, London, Faber & Faber.

National Curriculum Council (1990a), *Curriculum Guidance III: the whole curriculum*, York, National Curriculum Council.

National Curriculum Council (1990b) *Curriculum Guidance IV: education for economic and industrial understanding*, York, National Curriculum Council.

Peterson A. D. C. (1968), *The Future of Education*, London, Cresset Press.

Porter M. (1990), *The Competitive Advantage of Nations*, London, MacMillan.

Taylor W. (1985), 'Productivity and educational values'. In G. D. N. Worswick (ed.), *Education and Economic Performance*, London, Gower.

Taylor W. (1990), *Policy and Strategy in Higher Education* (collaboration between business and higher education), London, Department of Trade and Industry and Council for Industry and Higher Education.

Training Agency (1990), *Labour Market and Skill Trends 1991–92*, Sheffield, Training Agency.

Willoughby K. W. (ed.) (1990), *Technology Choice: a critique of the appropriate technology movement*, London, Intermediate Technology.

4

Beyond practice and theory: the domains of information technology in a changing world

RONALD K. GOODENOW

The British novelist David Lodge reminds us in *Nice Work*[1] that the lines between academic and industrial values are indeed fuzzy; not nearly as shocking as people from either side would have us believe. In *Small World*[2] he noted that with American Express and telephone credit cards anyone could turn attending international conferences into a full-time avocation, albeit at a delayed and ultimately high price. There are new tools of the trade: they include fax machines, modems and laptop computers. I am sure that somewhere in the world one of Lodge's radical literary deconstructionists is hooked up to a corporate official via any one of the hundreds of networks which are making the world a much different place – if not discussing the workplace they may be exchanging data on personal investment strategies. We are in a position to learn a great deal about technological tools of the educational trade and, hopefully, where both technology and changing educational policies and practices are taking us. My purpose is neither to dwell on technology nor describe good practice but instead to consider issues of domain. My perspective is derived from twenty years of academic endeavour in areas of educational reform, comparative studies and, now, both academic and industrial work on technology and knowledge transfer.

PROBLEMS IN SEARCH OF A SOLUTION

Larry Cuban of Stanford University points out in his excellent little book, *Teachers and Machines: the Classroom Use of Technology Since 1920*,[3] that classroom practice in the USA has changed but little since the nineteenth century in spite of the waves of new 'technologies' put in front of willing educators.

Though this observation may still hold true in many classrooms, there are signs everywhere of fundamental shifts; partly because of the technology and partly because the world itself is undergoing rapid and fundamental transitions. As put in a survey of educational practices by a computer magazine,[4] we are in the midst of: 'a quiet revolution . . . of phosphor, integrated circuits, and carrier tones . . . fueled by computer conferencing systems, modems, and on-line databases – the counterparts of yesteryear's chalkboards, lecture halls, and libraries'.

For signs of this change we need not look to the legions on the cutting edge of the information-technology revolution. As literary scholar Cecelia Tichi of Boston University writes in *Shifting Gears: technology, literature, culture in modernist America*:[5]

> The technology of girders and gears is no longer the dominant or defining technology. That position belongs to the computer. Even popular slang underscores the change. An eccentric or crazy individual formerly had a 'screw loose'; he or she now has a 'bad chip' . . . Behind the shift of images are new, technological definitions of the human relation to the world.

At a more macro level we know that the application of computer-based technologies to education is becoming a major policy issue in many nations. In some of the so-called developed countries, as in the case of Britain and the USA, there are serious efforts to integrate knowledge of them into national and state curricula. For developing ones, information technologies, in particular, offer an opportunity to overcome domestic and international isolation, create and transmit new (e.g. machine readable) forms of information and knowledge, and manage educational systems more efficiently. Indeed, as put by Henry T. Ingle, in an essay published in the *International Review of Education*:[6] 'The practice, theory, and research of the past 75 years in educational technology are converging to argue convincingly for the use of communication technologies – both existing and evolving – to achieve advances in the field of education and for related socio-economic development needs.'

The availability of international packet switching, the production of new and durable portable computers, efforts to create common international communications standards and operating systems, and the growing acceptance of computer- and video-based distance-learning programmes (e.g. recent Commonwealth Universities proposals) suggest that much of the world will share in what many writers have called a 'new information age'. This new age is one of sharing, communication, group work, of transcending old and defining new domains, of new forms of international relations.

When seen in global terms there are many impediments on the road to this new age. Many in the information technology industry have historical and moral concerns. We know that we must constantly think beyond profit to the ethical and proper use of what we make. As with many of the products of industrialism that are now falling by the wayside we cannot assume long-term prosperity and acceptance without addressing the full power and implications of what we make and sell in cultural terms. We cannot be truly responsible unless we look beyond the next innovation, the next product, today's market, the temptation to address only quarterly returns.

There are some broad problems. Firstly, a relative handful of nations still dominate the production and transfer of computers, software and communications systems – and how we think about them. Our multinationals must be more cross-culturally alert and integrated, and have a global perspective.[7] This perspective must transcend some of the conventional wisdom about 'globalisation'. We need a tough-minded understanding of patterns of dependency and interdependency among users and nations, and what constitutes social responsibility in a rapidly changing world. We need to find ways to understand and incorporate research on these issues.

In a world undergoing democratic change it is crucial that information technology serves demographic ends. Yet many university-to-university programmes and communications networks are constrainingly horizontal. They too seldom reach down and out to schools and the world of labour (or reach up to research scholars, scientists and policy people), and they exist primarily in the industrialised nations. In the non-industrialised world there is still concern that the old information order means cultural domination, and the new one will simply exploit human and other resources at greater velocity. Technology is too often applied differentially and without due consideration of ethnic, national or gender issues, visibly contributing its part to the structural inequalities which still plague our educational systems and societies. There are also many cultural barriers to effective technology use –

within organisations and the world at large – and we have a scant comparative perspective on either.

Openness and democratic objectives are also inhibited by the fact that protocols and systems have been developed too often, not by educators, but out of military or multinational corporate need; and in education, as in many other areas there is a towering and inscrutable babble of networks, databases and information architectures which blur what we do and what we need to do. Educators need to become far more familiar with advanced technologies and to let us know what they need to improve dramatically the quality of instruction and the educational workplace. We need to drive international standards, and commonly accessible databases and networks.

More active participation by teacher educators, teachers and other users will also help get the development of software and hardware in harmony both with educational need and each other – a major challenge. Many products and programmes are introduced not only before requisite training, but as Cuban points out, before critical issues of planning, psychology, organisational context and even power are addressed; too much is implemented from the top down without due involvement of teachers and children – a problem in other types of organisations as well – and too many of our strategies are devoid of cross-disciplinary understanding, serious thought, and, as many critics note, feeling.

We need to struggle with the fact that costs are high and perhaps intolerably so in the face of difficult economic conditions in many nations. Far more must be done to understand the relationship between cost and effectiveness, and educators must confront this boldly. We know what a computer can do for teacher or professor X or even department Y, but were the right investments made? Did the company selling the computer know the environment? Did the professors selecting the equipment know the software and hardware? Was there a firm institutional policy for investment, evaluation and return in place? There is nothing sadder in these difficult economic times than rooms filled with unused technology when children in many parts of the world need pens, pencils and a breakfast.

Finally, amidst considerable promise, hyperbole, confusion, and disappointment what is known about the application of computer-based technologies to education? Beyond formal studies on the numbers of computers supposedly used in the nations of the world (e.g. the work of the Evaluation Research Society) and many very confined studies about particular applications, what do we actually know about why educators use new technologies, why they resist them, what they do with them? Do we have a coherent and appropriate set of research studies to call on? Do we know what works and doesn't work, what impacts achievement positively, or negatively? Is there any consensus on research methodologies that are required to answer these questions, and do so comparatively? The temptation, in the US, at least, is to leave a lot of the 'interdisciplinary' knowledge of how computers work in organisations to loose coalitions of engineers and people from business schools.

These are some of the problems. One way to solve them is to develop a picture of the world in which we want to live, and to link technological visions to it. In this time of massive, and positive, global geopolitical change, there is reason to be optimistic because we are now forced to think creatively and with hope about the domains which will character-ise life on this planet in the early twenty-first century.

Those of us who see technology, not as panacea, but as a tool for empowerment, enrichment and bridge building must not be smug, however. There are many signs of neo-luddism as computers become equated with panacea solutions or the impersonality of modern bureauc-racy and crude attempts at modern-day Taylorism. More than a few critics are worrying aloud, in Lewis Mumford's terms, about the panop-ticon society of long-past 1984 and technology itself has many black eyes these days thanks to Chernobyl, Sellafield and Three Mile Island, the destruction of the ozone layer and runaway high-tech arms selling. Thoughtful writers, such as Alvin Weinberg in a recent issue of Minerva,[8] asked 'whether modern technology and democracy can coexist'. Vallee and Naisbitt answer in the affirmative, seeing new technologies as forcing a shift from hardened hierarchies to flexible and dynamic networks which change in the face of demand. Though Naisbitt anticipates a shift from 'representative' to more popular expressions of democracy, Vallee[9] reminds us that there is a battle for the soul of information technology between those who stand for what he calls the 'digital society' dominated by numbers and restricted choice and a fully participatory 'grapevine alternative'.

We now have an opportunity, indeed an obligation, to think through these issues and choices. At a very fundamental level we must mull over some key issues which are, in the words of Michael Rice:[10]

> To what extent are we using these systems to say and do what we want? And to what extent are we pulled toward using them in line with how they most effectively perform. A crucial aspect of that question is whether

advanced communications tend to be congenial or hostile to democratic values, or whether they will be important to the future of democracy purely according to how we decide they will be.

SOLUTIONS IN A WORLD OF CHANGE

The quest for solutions begins with the recognition that we *are* living in a time of paradigm shift, in technology and in world affairs. It would be an error to not look for interconnections. Some questions and issues need to be raised. Are we thinking about the implications of paradigm shifts *within* the domain of information technology itself?

Though there continue to be enormous changes in hardware – the stuff of information technology – and in such areas as artificial intelligence, people in industry and education are focusing increasingly on what I will call for lack of a better term, the 'second information technology revolution' wherein communication – within the local area networks of organisations and wide area networks which reach out around the world – is transcending stand-alone computing. This leads us to the domains within which there is important new work to be done.

Are we thinking about the educational workplace? There is a growing and fascinating new emphasis, more in American industry than in education, on the character of the workplace, and in the role of technology in preparing people for work, for organising work, for defining the nature of information sharing and decision making, and finally, hastening what Rosabeth Kanter and others refer to as the 'new managerial revolution'.[11] From my perspective at Digital, I see a dramatic increase in concern about these issues. Digital is sponsoring new research on such subjects as how people who work for small manufacturing concerns in rural areas of the American south view the value of technology to their labour and how information architectures develop against changing organisational values in a time of rapid manufacturing, technical and competitive advances. The conventional wisdom about knowing customers is true in highly complex ways that require new forms of understanding about how people, technology, work, and knowledge intersect. We need to know about this intersection for obvious reasons. As information technology becomes more ubiquitous and diffused across an educational or other enterprise, distinctions between hardware product sets become less important than such things as applications and how hardware is hooked up in networks. As consumers look more closely at their investment in information technology they are becoming more critical of what their investment in machines, applications and networks can produce – and what it means in terms of organisational readiness to use them. One can have all the wonderful machines and applications in the world and still fail because of poor management and inadequate knowledge of human factors.

There are some positive signs for education here, however. Though the research base remains pretty thin, it is possible to say, in the USA at least, that just as shifting modes of production, and management impacted on organisations in the early years of this century[12] – moving us in the direction of the bureaucratic-hierarchical organisations with which we are all very familiar – the second revolution in information technology is transforming the domain of work. Though it is possible to over-simplify, the implications of this are very progressive, requiring a great deal of open communication and sharing; a new workplace environment within which people work with knowledge far differently. We must, in sum, look at our schools and universities as workplaces, and understand the implications of information technology for them as such. Indeed, understanding the relationship between technology and educational work is a major new challenge for educational researchers, who have done very little work on the topic.

It is not irrelevant, moreover, that in the USA, as in Britain, there is considerable energy devoted to determining how education might better relate to the larger world of work; and how technology might improve and drive this relationship so that we meet our future human resource requirements (not only of the computer industry), and so technology is a tool for empowerment, not alienation. Once we know more about attitudes in the rural south, for example, we can begin to apply our wonderful networking technology to creating bridges between schooling and work that help provide relevancy and stimulation to large numbers of students now largely unserved by our schools. Indeed, in such programmes as Digital's DEC College programme here in Britain, one can see the breakdown of many barriers between the educational sector and the high-technology workplace.

Work and workplaces, however, cannot be divorced in our changing world, from the issue of community. This new emphasis on communication, and on interaction, on communities that can be built around computer networks, constitutes another domain of enormous promise, one that is clearly linked to the first. Worldwide, as anyone who uses the academic networks knows, are hundreds of new communities of people who share their ideas and lives. Having attended, here in London and in New York, the past two conferences of the Global Educational Telecommunications Network (GETN), and working for a company that has a huge international network which links people up in notesfiles on everything from technology, to fishing to finding a bed and breakfast in Yorkshire, this technology can indeed build new communities and meet educational objectives in powerful ways. Indeed, if we look critically at the institutional and psychological factors that contribute to the isolation and loneliness of teachers we can create enduring and powerful new support networks to enhance effectiveness; and break down barriers of distance in doing so. It is easy and cheap for a teacher from the Outer Hebrides to find him or herself in the middle of New York thanks simply to the Times Network for Schools and a packet switch through Dialcom.

To build enduring communities, however, we must fully understand the 'activity' in which we are involved and within which we link technology to larger sets of community objectives. It is one thing to build something called communities, it is another to do so within the context of how we think social and economic life is being ordered in a rapidly changing world – and how the school should socialise young people to be prepared to act democratically and effectively in that world. We must know what the computer can do and what it cannot do. We must move it from a tool for rote and drill, to one that fosters interaction, exploration, creativity, and working in groups. Hence, in the school, we must be sure that our networking and communications projects – whether within institutions or between them – do not merely foster old hierarchies and top-down solutions.

This issue is directly relevant in a time when educational 'reform' is much on the agenda in the US and Britain. If, as in the words of psychologist Michael Cole to the American Educational Research Association,[13] the computer is a 'mediational technology . . . a general purpose tool for the manipulation of information and . . . a medium for pursuing educational goals that have nothing intrinsically to do with computer programming', we need to understand what role technology can play in creating reforms that reflect our conceptions of community, and the potential for creativity, excitement and empowerment that is present in modern technologies. We would be making a dreadful mistake if we merely used technology to reinforce ideas of efficiency, productivity, and social relations derived from an earlier age. The context for this 'reform' is therefore greater than the school; it is linked to where the world is going in the last years of this century.

The next domain is one that is truly exciting. It involves the global transitions which we witness daily. There are shifts to democracy in many parts of the world – who would have thought that the East

German army would now be part of NATO? We see a growing attention to the post-cold war world and meeting in concert its global problems of resources and environment. There is a growing emphasis on 'cultural' as opposed to military or sheer financial capital, and the desire in most parts of the world to strike a new balance between capitalism and socialism, with the balance tilting heavily in the direction of free markets, free ideas, travel, and, for our purposes, global networks that make the work of Arthur Clarke and other so-called science fiction writers truly prophetic.

Critically we must consider where we are in terms of new forms of educational and cultural relations – and transforming, with the help of technology, the international order. We are not only examining such things as industry-school partnerships and relations, or 'technology transfer' to meet our goals. We should be looking at how we, as educators, can play a role in the cultural relationships, the technological relationships, which are building a new international order based on our visions. How can we use the technologies to further the goal of creating an international domain of learning, teaching, researching and transferring? What tools, methodologies, skills, and attitudes will be required? My personal research on international educational relations[14] suggest that this is a subject about which we actually know little; as a subset of cultural relations it is virgin territory for research and new relationships that transcend those which, as in the past, have usually included contacts between elites. Children, teachers, computer programmers, software engineers, ordinary professors in faraway places can now, thanks to interactive technologies, become more of the 'stuff' of international relations. If we are intelligent about this, and communicate well, perhaps our leaders will learn something from us!

The opportunities facing us then, are exciting. How, with the power of international communications networks, interactive video, and many of the other tools at our disposal do we help shape this order? How do we overcome our parochialisms (our 'industrial perspective', or our more genteel 'academic perspective')? What can we share from our experiences with curriculum reform and the role of technology in it; an issue with which many have been struggling in Britain? How can our companies, and our companies within companies, learn from educators, from each other, from serious research and scholarship on technology in education? How do we use technology to create new networks that are vertical, sharing, and far more democratic than the highly stratified communication which has typified education in the past? Or, will we enter the twenty-first century with nineteenth-century classrooms?

NOTES

1 David Lodge (1988), *Nice Work*, London, Penguin.
2 David Lodge (1985) *Small World*, London, Penguin.
3 Larry Cuban (1987), *Teachers and Machines: the classroom use of technology since 1920*, New York, College Press.
4 Brock N. Meeks (1987), 'The quiet revolution: on-line education becomes a real alternative', *Byte* February, p. 183.
5 Cecelia Tichi, (1987) *Shifting Gears: technology, literature, culture in modernist America*, Chapel Hill and London, University of North Carolina Press, pp. xi-xii.
6 See Henry T. Ingle (1986), 'New media, old media: the technologies of international development', *International Review of Education*, 32 pp. 251–68.
7 See R. Murray Thomas and Victor N. Kobayashi (1987), *Educational Technology: its creation, development and cross-cultural transfer*, Oxford, Pergamon Press.
8 Alvin M. Weinberg (1990), 'Technology and democracy', *Minerva*, spring p. 81. See also Lewis Mumford (1967), *The Myth of the Machine*, London: Secker & Warburg.
9 See J. Vallee (1987), *The Network Revolution: confessions of a computer scientist*, (Berkeley And/Or Press, p. 54; and J. Naisbitt (1984), *Megatrends*, New York, Warner Books.
10 Michael Rice (1985), 'The future for democracy in an age of changing communications', *Communications and Society Forum Report*, the Aspen Institute, Queenstown, Maryland, p. 8.
11 For useful overviews see Rosabeth Moss Kanter, (1989), 'The new managerial work', *Harvard Business Review*, November-December, pp. 85–92; Shoshanna Zuboff (1988), *In the Age of the Smart Machine*, New York, Basic Books; Charles M. Savage (1990), *Fifth Generation Management: integrating enterprises through human network*, Bedford, Mass., Digital Press; and Marvin R. Weisbord (1989), *Productive Workplaces*, San Francisco, Jossey-Bass.
12 For a valuable historical interpretation of how these changes impacted American education early in this century, see David B. Tyack (1974), *The One Best System: a history of American urban education*, Cambridge, Harvard University Press. I have looked at some international implications of these changes in Ronald K. Goodenow (1984), 'Transcending the legacy of twentieth-century American schooling: in search of a global perspective', *Issues in Education*, summer, pp. 44–55. For questions about how ideas on educational work and change are transferred internationally see Ronald K. Goodenow (1992) 'Problematics and domains: thinking internationally about urban education'. In Ronald K. Goodenow and William Marsden, (eds), (1992), *The City and Education in Four Nations*, Cambridge, Cambridge University Press.
13 Michael Cole (1990), 'Computers and the organization of new forms of educational activity: a socio-historical perspective', paper presented at the meetings of the American Educational Research Association, Boston, 18 April p. 21.
14 See Ronald K. Goodenow (1990), 'John Dewey and American progressive education in the third world', *History of Education*, January, pp. 23–40.

5

The challenge from industry

DAVID WOOLDRIDGE

This chapter is written from the perspective of a vice president of a large technological corporation, which has to cope with the dramatic speed of technological change. I aim to show that the education system is in deep crisis, and to argue that American industry has been sitting on the sideline for too long with regard to this and to the community which it serves. People are ignoring what is happening to society as a result of technology and unless action is taken quickly then the problems will multiply.

The speed of technological change has been, and continues to be, dramatic and accelerating. Today everything is a system and it is the convergence of technologies which is the key to success. In Motorola this is called the four Cs, i.e. the coming together of communications, components, computing and control. We are now totally dependent on information and the technology required to communicate and manipulate that information. Emerging technology will soon see systems capable of the transfer of images and even 3D motion to a variety of mobile receivers and transmitters all linked to the same system. Motorola foresees the day when voice communication will represent just 5 per cent of the total global communications industry. These changes place new pressure and increased difficulties on marketing tasks for corporations such as Motorola's. Technology for technology's sake is no longer as important as the marketing of technological products. Technology is now available to everyone and this makes market dominance, for corporations such as Motorola more difficult to achieve. It is no longer a single-product industry but one which requires thorough understanding of the convergence of not only current technologies but also emerging technologies.

Product development cycles are often shorter than selling gestation periods creating problems of obsolescence before those products can be made available to the market. This means that our customers are demanding migration paths and long-term capabilities. Price is a much bigger issue due to increased competition and reduced production costs made possible through advances in technology. For customers, the purchasing decisions have become more complex because of competing technologies, product obsolescence risks and their lack of knowledge of technological developments.

Similarly achieving customer satisfaction is more difficult because:

1 There are more options available in purchasing decisions.
2 There is increased competition, and technology is driving up customer expectations.
3 Quality and price now form a larger part of buyer consideration.
4 Systems implementations are more difficult to realise due to increased software content.
5 Product and system enhancements are easier to come by and fast paced technology changes are creating the need for migration paths.

It is apparent that there is an increasing requirement for a new partnership with our customers. We need to keep customers informed of our long-range strategies and the technologies we are developing. A total system capability is an important consideration over black-box products, and consequently it becomes more important for us to know and understand the total customer environments. To the customer there is no clear separation between competitors and allies. To industry it is survival of the fittest, and future success will depend on keeping pace and staying ahead in the technology race.

The corporate impact of these changes is considerable, which leads to a need to operate at minimum costs and maximum quality in order to provide customer satisfaction at competitive prices. This demands two prerequisites:

1 An increase in the investment in research and development.
2 A world-class workforce capable of high performance within flexible work teams.

This will place increased pressure on engineering organisations as the degree of specialisation becomes greater and the generalist becomes less effective. However this type of workforce is more difficult to manage. It must have more in-depth technical knowledge with a broader understanding of many areas of specialisation. There is ever-increasing difficulty in keeping pace with rapid changes in technology.

Corporations will need vastly improved marketing skills with a thorough understanding of emerging technologies and anticipation of technology changes. There will need to be a decreased cycle time in all aspects of business, especially delivery and product development. They must be capable of producing systems over the required marketing period and product development cycles must get shorter and shorter if they are not to be obsolete by the time they are put on the market. This leads to a need to develop improved technical selling organisations and a much bigger investment in education and training.

Why are corporate executives concerned? The short answer is that the education system is failing to respond to these needs of industry, which can be illustrated by referring to some background statistics. A recent survey in the US showed that during an average week an 8th grader spends 21.4 hours watching television, 5.6 hours of homework and just 1.8 hours of outside reading. It showed that less than 40 per cent of 17-year olds possess adept reading skills and only 20 per cent do an adequate job of writing a letter, and concludes that a third of all students are unprepared for productive lives.

Worldwide, US students rank 49th out of 158 in literacy, 29 per cent of high-school students drop out of school and only 15 per cent of high-school entrants complete college. In 1977 there were 4 million high school sophomores, and in 1992 the number of Ph.D. degrees in science and engineering will be just 9,700. Motorola estimates the demand to be of the order of 20,000. The concerns can be summarised by four converging trends in the USA:

1 Population growth rate is declining and hence there is a shrinking number of 16- to 22-year olds entering the workforce and entering college.
2 Jobs are requiring higher levels of knowledge and skills.
3 Student achievement has not increased significantly and, by some if not most indicators, has sharply declined over the past twenty years.
4 Minority students, who are least well served by the school system, are the fastest-growing segments of the population.

This raises the question as to how a competitive edge can be gained in the global marketplace under these conditions? Corporate executives put forward the view that the education system is now threatening their survival and it is time to become more involved with raising academic standards before it is too late. They argue that those corporations which do not become involved will inevitably lose their competitiveness and fail to respond to the changes in technology. Higher education is too important to be left to the teachers and its administrators; industry and the community must become involved now before it is too late.

This is the challenge to education, and in preparing new graduate engineers for industry there is a need for more hands-on projects which provide the skills necessary to work on relevant design problems and to develop those troubleshooting skills needed by industry. Those graduates must be able to handle test equipment which will be used in a variety of systems. They must be able to learn to define their own requirements and can resolve their own deficiencies in design and requirements definition.

We need more training in structured methods, more computer science in the curriculum and a better understanding of design for quality and manufacturability. Motorola's own initiative is the creation of the Motorola University with the following mission: 'To anticipate and meet the training needs of the corporation, to enhance individual competence, improve organisational performance. We will train Motorolans and selected key suppliers and customers worldwide.'

It offers a wide range of training and education programmes to respond to the needs of both Motorola and its customers by providing specialist courses which combine technology with business and management. Programmes are usually project driven with close liaison with customers to ensure that customer requirements are fully understood.

We believe that the way forward is a proper collaborative approach between industry and education in which industry plays an active role in developing the school curriculum and in making teachers aware of the particular needs of industry and of technology changes. Only if there is an active participation in all aspects of the education system by corporations such as mine will we be in a position to respond to the changes we are facing in respect of technological advance. This is a challenge to us all and, in particular, the challenge to industry.

6

The response of the higher education system to the challenge

JOHN ASHWORTH

The past decades have witnessed a noticeable decline in the UK manu-facturing industry. What started out slowly in the 1950s and 1960s has accelerated over the last twenty years with the result that the UK is in a weak position compared to many other developed countries. What remains of the UK manufacturing industry is often controlled by interests outside the UK, as part of multinational corporations. Conse-quently, there is a lack of an autonomous UK industrial policy and this directly impinges on the role of the British higher-education system in research and development in these areas.

Although there remain a number of process industries controlled by the UK, many of these attract profits that are drawn from outside the UK and once again this provides an unavoidable international dimension. The story is not, however, all gloom and doom because there is an increasing window of opportunity for work of components industries and this opportunity is being taken by a number of new and existing companies. However, a common feature of these organisations is that they are classed as small firms in comparison to the manufactur-ing giants of the past. These organisations and the remaining manufac-turing and process industries will need to invest heavily in research and development, in particular, the application of new and information technology if they are to remain competitive with their overseas equiva-lents.

The international dimension also requires that staff in these organis-ations need to communicate effectively with customers, suppliers and competitors from overseas. Not only should they be familiar and comfortable with the latest forms of communication technology, such as electronic mail, but they should also be able to communicate effec-tively in languages additional to their native English. Any training that they receive should address, in the former case, the organisational impact of E-mail as well as the technology behind it, and in the latter case the aspects of culture and business methods of the other countries as well as the language.

These needs were anticipated in the mid 1980s at Salford University and, following many consultations with industry and government, led to the setting up of the Information Technology (IT) Institute. The role of the institute is that of a centre of excellence in information technology and its application to the problems outlined above and it covers the range of activities from research and development, through specialist post-graduate and degree courses to short courses and consultancies. One of the key aspects of the mission of the institute is to build and maintain very close relationships with a range of industrial clients – clients of the output of all the activities of the Institute.

What is needed, I believe, is a recognition of the needs of the user community; a radical review of the balance of education and training provided and provision of courses which do not necessarily require good A-level maths and physics as prerequisites. It was with a view to providing just such courses that the University of Salford, approached the National Computing Centre (NCC), in the summer of 1984. I proposed that we jointly approached government and industry with a view to setting up an information technology institute which would be run as a collaborative venture by the parties concerned. After much to-ing and fro-ing and after drastically scaling down the size of our proposed Institute – so that it fitted the money available from government rather than meeting the need we saw for student places – this institute has now been established. We received £1.43 million of public funds over the three years 1984–7 with a similar contribution from a variety of industrial collaborators including supplier companies (such as Rank Xerox, IBM, Sperry, Prime, GEC, Ferranti, DEC, CAP) as well as user organisations (such as ICI, British Aerospace, British Gas, BNFL, Littlewoods, Unipart). It is, however, essential for the success of the Institute for such initial support to be followed up by the establishment of a close working relationship. The university has established appropriate mechanisms to ensure that such an industrial/commercial involvement becomes a reality.

Collaboration is not only required between industrial/commercial partners and the University, but also between the industrial/commercial partners themselves. No single organisation is currently offering a majority of the support, so that considerable goodwill and flexibility is needed to resolve issues of course curriculum (which databases? which

mail systems? which fourth-generation languages?) and hardware provision (which peripheral devices? what communications network? which
mainframe access?). Such cooperation can also prove useful to the
industrial/commercial partners.

The main B.Sc. degree is different form those usually offered in universities and polytechnics in several ways. Firstly, industrialists at all levels,
including managers working with graduates and those responsible for
interviewing and recruiting graduates, have made clear their belief that
universities and polytechnics can and should do more to ensure better
development of the qualities, skills and abilities relevant to employment,
within the framework of degree programmes. The Institute responds to
their list of desirable qualities, skills and abilities which includes:

1   An appreciation of and empathy for the nature, methodologies, aims
    and objectives of business.
2   The personal/interpersonal skills and abilities essential for making
    effective contributions to an organisation. These include:
    • the ability to tackle open-ended problems;
    • the communication skills essential for working in teams;
    • the ability to adjust quickly to change (the rate of introduction of
      new technologies in order to maintain competitiveness puts a
      premium on the ability of members of a workforce to respond by
      acquiring and applying new knowledge and skills).
3   The confidence needed to establish and maintain a high level of
    personal productivity – that is, confidence resulting from successful
    experience in uncertain situations.

Secondly, the Institute recognised that the pool of students with good
grades in A-level mathematics and physics is very limited, and industrial
experience has shown that many areas of IT-related work can be
handled very successfully by a numerate and literate graduate who
nevertheless lacks both an A-level and university or polytechnic training
in these subjects. Further support for this view results from the experience of the NCC in its Threshold Scheme and also by the reports from
the Institute for Manpower Studies on the success of arts graduates
taking IT conversion courses.

There are far more students failing to obtain university and polytechnic places with excellent A-level grades in the arts than there are in the
sciences and there is also a very strong demand for degrees involving
business studies, either alone or in combination with other subjects.
Thus the IT Institute sets out to attract students with good A-levels
(or equivalent qualifications) in *any* subjects.

The university recognised that if it is to attract students from a

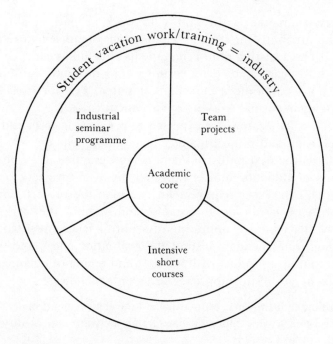

6.1 Structure of the IT Institute

broad background into an IT course then it must mount a substantial marketing effort; it will be particularly important to attract women, and in this regard the collaboration of the Equal Opportunities Commission has been secured. A number of other outside agencies also help in the mounting of a substantial publicity campaign.

Thirdly, the Institute recognised that a conventional university degree course does not necessarily increase the level of fitness for employment of students in terms of the abilities and skills outlined earlier. For most of those who have taken a three-year full-time non-sandwich degree, entering employment represents a considerable culture shock. So, fulfilment of the objectives of the IT Institute requires a study programme which contributes to the shifting of a significant part of this initial learning curve into the period of study for the degree. The structure designed to achieve this (see Figure 6.1) consists of an academic core taught and assessed in a traditional manner, supplemented by four additional teaching/training features: team projects, an industrial seminar programme (seminars presented by speakers from industry/commerce), intensive short courses, and industrial placements during vacations.

One attribute which is seen as important in fitting graduates for work in industry/commerce is the ability to work as part of a team. To develop this attribute, the student population is organised into a number of teams, each consisting of fifteen students (five first-year, five second-year, five third-year). Each team occupies a 'team-room', equipped with a workstation containing a personal computer (PC) for each student. This forms their normal working environment.

Industrial collaborators are expected to prepare projects and to help with supervision and project management which is modelled as closely as possible on the best industrial/commercial practice. Each team contains a mix of students, and is expected, for each project, to identify and document the 'user requirements', to plan the project, with milestones and demonstrations, to organise and monitor the work of each member of the team, to apply quality-control techniques (structured walk-throughs, independent testing and evaluation, etc.), and to 'package' the results as a product with full user and reference documentation.

The advantages of this approach are seen as follows:

- Training to team work, estimating and the achievements of deadlines.
- Exercise of a wide range of managerial, software and literary skills in the project work.
- Informal training of first-year students by third-year students.
- Continuity of operation from year to year, extending into links between employed graduates and their erstwhile project team.
- Development of the ability to undertake complex and open-ended investigations.

Seminars on a wide variety of practical topics provide insight into essential differences between real-world problems and those included in academic courses at undergraduate level: for example, in terms of scale and complexity. Insight is also gained into the way in which industrial and commercial organisations deal with such problems, in why the problems are important, into business imperatives (which demand economical solutions) and so on.

The seminars given in any particular year are organised so that there is a common theme or themes running through them (supportive of the academic core lectures). Each seminar is followed by questions to the speaker, discussions (led by a member of staff) in each of the team rooms, and a written report produced jointly by the team. The report includes not only factual material, but also attempts to relate the seminar to other seminars or lecture material, and suggests possible answers to any problems raised by the speaker.

Two types of short courses are included. One type involves use of computer-based teaching methods in order to provide specific skills. The other type is modelled on 'State-of-the-art' presentations provided commercially and utilising high-quality visual aids, substantial course notes and reference materials. In both cases students gain experience of industrial training methods and some of the techniques by which employees in industrial organisations gain state-of-the-art information and skills. For some areas of teaching (e.g. communications), Institute staff are expected to have sufficient recognition, as international experts, and sufficient experience with giving this type of course, both to prepare the material and to present the course. In other areas (e.g. graphics), staff in the university have the necessary expertise for course design and preparation. In yet other areas, the university is able to obtain detailed assistance from collaborators with material, advice, preparation, or even presentation of courses.

The placements are an important source of contacts and initial work on team projects, but most importantly they bring a recognition and empathy for business aims, objectives and procedures. It is seen as essential to obtain placement of all students during their two long summer vacations with collaborating firms. This is often linked to sponsorship of students, thus resulting in a close relationship and developing empathy between the student and the business world. The nature of the student intake results in some students, perhaps a significant number, having an A level in French or German (for example). We recognise the importance of not allowing such a language skill to lapse, and of the value of such a skill to an IT graduate. The aim is (as a minimum) to obtain placements for long vacation work with the European laboratories and offices of IT Institute collaborators for such students. This idea is currently being extended to include tuition in languages for all students, regardless of their entry qualifications. By this means, all students graduating from the Institute will be able to fulfil the requirements imposed by the international dimension described in the earlier part of the paper.

The Institute has undertaken careful monitoring and evaluation of its activities since its inception. The results of this are extremely encouraging and support many of the assumptions made during the inauguration of the Institute. The results support the view that a science background is not a prerequisite for success in the field of information technology. The development of language skills in the students enhance their marketability on graduation. The increasing number of mature students enrolling on the degree programme has also demonstrated the ability to be successful, despite finding some of the early stages of the course more difficult when compared with the experiences of the younger students. The experiments in using the technology to drive parts of the assessment process have been very successful and help to build a comprehensive profile of the students' abilities. Finally, it has been found that the aptitude tests widely used for selection in the IT industry were not particularly successful pointers to the potential of students but that some of the various tests on personality and interpersonal skills look to be much better predictors, and further interesting work is being done in this area by the Institute.

7

Partnership between education and business

SIR ADRIAN CADBURY

That the relationship between education and business should be one of partnership seems both sensible and natural. School children move from the world of education to the world of work and while the term business does not cover all types of work, it covers the majority of the careers which they will undertake. The essential point is that school pupils and company employees are the same people; the difference is one of timing. In order that this progression from school to work should be as straight-forward and as productive, from the point of view of the individuals, as possible, there needs to be an effective partnership between education and business. Given that a partnership of this nature is so clearly to the advantage of all concerned, why in this country, at least, has there been such a gulf between the worlds of education and of work? I do not intend to devote space unnecessarily to the past, but we can only put the partnership concept into context, if we have some feel for the historical gap between business and education. The aims of higher education in this country in the nineteenth century can be, perhaps unfairly summed up by this quotation from a sermon preached by the Rev. Thomas Gaisford, one Good Friday: 'The advantages of a classical education are twofold. It enables us to look down with contempt on those who have not shared its advantages and also fits us for places of emolument, not only in this world but in that which is to come'. I have to point out without any Cambridge bias, that he was the Regius Prof. of Greek in the University of Oxford. I cannot help wondering what his parishioners, who had not shared his advantages, made of it all. In a curious way, the Gaisford view of education was totally vocational, within a framework which recognised the Church as the sole vocation.

The consequences of an educational approach which saw no relationship between education and earning a living were aptly described by Herbert Spencer, writing in 1869:

> That which our School Courses leave almost entirely out, we thus find to be what most nearly concerns the business of life. Our industries would cease were it not for the information which men acquire, as best they may, after their education is said to be finished. The vital knowledge – that by which we have grown as a nation to what we are and which now underlies our whole existence – is a knowledge that has got itself taught in nooks and corners, while the ordained agencies for teaching have been mumbling little else but dead formulae.

The reaction of those in business who had acquired their useful knowledge in nook and corners was an unfortunate, if understandable, contempt for the educational system and for its products, and a far too exclusive reliance on the experience of practical men. The lack of respect for technik (or even a word for it), which the Germans ranked alongside the arts and the sciences and saw as a bridge between them, has cost business and the nation dear in competitive terms.

As a final illustration, here is what the senior pupils of my old school, writing at about the same time as Herbert Spencer, had to say on the introduction of French into the curriculum:

> So great a part of the French vocabulary consists of Latin words corrupted or disguised, that a knowledge of the latter language, we had almost said, is equivalent to a certain proficiency in the former. This being the case, would it not be a manifest waste of valuable time, to devote a laborious course of tuition to that for which a dictionary and a few brains would be sufficient? But apart from these considerations, it is at least a matter of question, whether the intrinsic merits of French literature are such as to justify the sacrifice of any considerable and definite portion of time in the routine of school-work, to the study of composition in that tongue. Artificial and shallow, the productions of French authors are very generally an exact reflex of the national character. At any rate, experience has shown that it is little short of Quixotic to aim at acquiring a correct French accent except by actual intercourse with natives, and by deriving pronunciation of words from those who use them every day of their lives.
>
> It is for these reasons that we hope that French will not be suffered to fill too large a space in the education of the School.

In effect, they were arguing that if you had received a scholarly education then you should be able to pick up anything useful to the business of life for yourself. It was in this manner that we built the divide between business and education, which we now have to bend all our efforts to bridging. That divide has been closing measurably, during my working life. There is still a view in business that the schools are out of touch with the world of work and with what it is that companies are looking for in their recruits. There is still a view in schools that all that employers want are young people who will willingly put up with boring, dead-end jobs. Now those suspicions will not vanish with the wave of the partnership wand. Some jobs are boring and some schools are out of touch, but the only people who can put them in touch are those with business experience who are willing to share it.

While partnership will not solve all the difficulties and misunderstandings between us, without it there will be no progress. The three forces which make that progress essential are the challenge of technology, the need to compete in the markets of the world and demography. It is, however, important to recognise that it was not just schools and companies which held each other at arm's length. The view of many parents was that a large part of business, that is to say manufacturing industry as opposed to the professions, had little that was acceptable to offer to their children in the way of a career. They saw education not as a way in to industry, in this rather limited sense, but as a means of escaping it.

This was the background to the UK's Industry Year 1986, which aimed to bring home to all the groups which make up our society, the degree to which the quality of our lives depended directly or indirectly on industry – I prefer where possible to substitute the word 'business' for 'industry', as I think that 'industry' gives a misleadingly narrow impression of what Herbert Spencer called the business of life. The need to mount a nationwide campaign of this sort, reflected the difference in the standing of business in this country, compared with its standing in the countries with which we compete. After all, every year is Industry Year in Japan.

Just as education had played an important part in *forming* our national attitudes towards business, so it had to play its part in *changing* them. That is why business-education partnerships were so central to Industry Year 1986 and to maintaining the momentum for change thereafter. The lessons to be learnt from the compact approach in the United States gave further support to the schools-business partnership approach in this country. There is no doubt about the partnership progress which was achieved under the auspices of Industry Year. In the Midlands, we moved from having a minority of secondary schools linked to companies to a position where the majority were so linked. One of the simplest ways of establishing links between business and education is through workshadowing, an initiative which provided the theme for David Lodge's novel, *Nice Work* – a book which may have aroused exaggerated expectations as to what workshadowing might lead to.

I had two shadows from a local school in 1986; I enjoyed their company and I learnt from them. They brought home to me what a poor job those of us in companies do to get across the inherent interest and challenge of working in the business of today. Both were surprised at the degree to which people on the shop floor, of the factories we visited, enjoyed what they were doing and took a pride in it. We need to project a far more vivid and challenging picture of what the world of work has to offer than we have done to date.

What we learnt, from our Industry Year efforts at linking, is that nothing happens until you establish personal contacts – teachers going into companies and people from companies going into schools. Directives and exhortations from above are a necessary part of the initiative, but of themselves they do not achieve a great deal. Much of the follow-up of the Colloquium (which has resulted in this book) and its capacity to turn ideas into action will depend on the individual partnerships which it will help to bring about.

Partnerships in action takes place at the local level and it is at the local level that the identity of interest between education and business is most apparent. Looking at the matter from the point of view of a local company talking to a local school the message would be: 'Many of your pupils will become our employees and many of our employees are the parents of your pupils. We are therefore, tied to each other and the test of the effectiveness of the partnership between us is the benefits which it will bring to individual pupils, as they move from the World of Education to the World of Work.'

While the implementation of partnerships has to be local, it needs to be possible to take full advantage of the whole range of services offered by national and regional bodies, which have been formed to support different aspects of the partnership approach – arrangements for work experience, the encouragement of enterprise activities and the provision by business of teaching materials, for example. Schools and companies which plan to work more closely together need to be able to draw on the experience of all those who have travelled the same road before them, and to know where to go for what kind of advice.

In summary, local action, if it is to make the best use of scarce resources, needs a national framework within which to work. The Foundation for Education and Business Partnerships was set up to provide just that framework. We are only too conscious as a foundation that we have not been formed to dictate to those organisations, who are already involved in serving the partnership cause, what they should be doing. We will only receive the support on which we depend as a foundation, provided that we are seen to add value to what is already happening on the ground. The foundation's value lies in its ability to appreciate all that is going on in the wide field of education-business links and through that appreciation to provide a sense of vision and framework of priorities for the partnership movement as a whole. Alongside vision and priorities goes values, we all have to be concerned not just with links between schools and companies but with the quality of those links.

The foundation has, therefore, to listen to those in the field and to be in touch not only with what is already happening, but with what is being proposed. It is an enabling organisation, encouraging the efforts of individuals on which all progress depends and helping them to ensure that their individual and collective efforts reinforce each other by working together towards common goals. One of those goals on the business side has to be to involve a far greater number of companies and a wider range of companies, (because I suspect that middle-sized companies are under-represented), in joint activities with schools. Another goal has to be for the partnership approach to reach down to the primary schools; that is the stage when the attention of children needs to be caught by the challenge of technology and the exciting opportunities which it presents.

The foundation also constitutes a natural way of bringing the third side of the triangle into the partnership – government. Government's interest in business-education partnerships, both nationally and locally, is self-evident. At the national level, it spans more than one department of state. At the same time, the decisions and actions of government have a considerable impact on the partnership approach. It is, therefore, of the highest importance that education, business and government should be aware of each other's aims and intentions and as far as possible co-ordinate them. The foundation provides a forum for sharing views and for improving understanding between the three prime movers in this broader partnership.

I am encouraged in general by the direction which educational change is taking, both in terms of the curriculum and in terms of the governance of schools. Economic awareness has been accepted as one of the cross-curricular themes in schools and in the training of teachers. On the governance side, the aim is to devolve more and more of the management of schools on to the schools themselves. These policy shifts offer a double opportunity to business. They give business a point of contact with what is being taught in schools and with the way in which schools are being run. Business can, therefore, help with teaching in schools, through the provision of course material and the setting up of joint projects, and at times the loan of staff, while business governors can bring with them the management skills for survival in an uncertain and competitive world, which schools will increasingly have to acquire to the same end. This convergence in educational and business aims will prove a fruitful source of partnership opportunities.

That brings me to what business and education might expect from working more closely with each other. An important element in the partnership is the concern which both schools and companies have that between us we do not do as good a job for those leaving education and entering employment as we would like. Companies and schools are based in the same communities and accept that they have responsibilities to those communities. At a more commercial level, no business is protected against international competition and that competition is increasingly based on knowledge and the use to which knowledge is put. The future of our companies, therefore, depends on the educational base of those who work in them and their ability to apply their knowledge to the world of work. We start in the UK from a low base in terms of the level of education and of qualifications of our workforce from the board room to the shop floor, compared with our main industrial competitors; so to compete internationally we have to raise our standards of education and training faster than they are doing. What is encouraging from the business side is how much is already being done within education to meet what business expects from the partnership approach. There are two general headings which summarise much of what industry is looking for from the schools: education for capability and enterprise education.

Education for Capability is the title of an initiative promoted by the RSA or, to give it its full title, the Royal Society for the Encouragement of Arts, Manufactures and Commerce. The RSA masterminded Industry Year and has always been an effective partnership organisation, serving both education and business through its schemes of training and qualifications. Education for Capability brought together a wide range of people who supported a change in educational direction. Put at its simplest, the approach to education is based on the 'enabling curriculum', which is designed to help and encourage everyone to show of what they are capable, as opposed to an educational system which labels pupils as being able, or more frequently unable, to pass certain limited tests – limited in the sense that they only test some of the capacities which individuals have and not necessarily those that are primarily relevant to their futures.

Perhaps the first point business is looking for under the education for capability heading is a wider view of achievement than the traditional examination system has provided. Companies are interested in every aspect of endeavour, not only academic endeavour, and are particularly concerned with the ability to work with others. Problems in business are rarely solved by individuals working on their own, as they are expected to do in traditional examinations, where collaboration is regarded as cheating. They are solved by team work and the ability to get the most out of a team is one of the key attributes for a successful industrial career. Companies are looking for people who have shown that they want to learn, can learn and intend to continue to learn throughout their lives. We are interested in what people have learnt, rather than what they have been taught. This, in turn, involves accepting the validity of learning from experience; not the narrow reliance on practical experience I referred to earlier, but the capacity to draw creatively on both knowledge *and* experience.

The next issue is how education for capability can be assessed. The frustration of educationalists is understandable when industry asks for methods of assessment which are more relevant to the careers they have to offer and then they (or their recruiters) fall back on selection by academic grades often quite inappropriately. That underlines the need for more interchange and the need to get people from business into schools to see what is going on and to understand the new pattern of qualifications. In fact, the introduction of GCSE, of A/S levels, of practical options in examinations and the preparation of profiles of what pupils have achieved as a means of assessment, are all indicators of the degree to which schools are moving down the education for capability road already.

Business believes too that schools would be helped by the involvement of outsiders with the aim of enabling pupils to become more aware of the links between their education and the world of work. This in turn should strengthen their motivation to learn and provide them with a basis on which to shape their own courses of study more confidently. In all this there does seem to me to be a fair degree of agreement within the educational profession about the direction in which education should go and is going. It is along education for capability lines and it means that the aims of business and education are converging.

The second heading to which I referred was education for enterprise. This is an aspect of education which is important to individual companies and to the nation as a whole. When I left university, I along with the overwhelming majority, expected to work for somebody else. This is not the outlook, for example, in the United States, where far more people take the risk of starting up on their own and if they fail put it down to experience and try again. We need more self-starters, because our companies are increasingly organised on the basis of business units run by small teams which are encouraged to operate entrepreneurially.

Nationally it is from the rise of small firms that new jobs will come and in terms of international competition it is small firms which have the ability to be quick on their feet and responsive to changing markets. A great deal is being done to encourage enterprise education in schools. In fact, the aim is to move on from including it in the secondary curriculum to offering it in all primary schools in the near future; so the schools are playing their part vigorously. From the business side there are organisations like Young Enterprise, which help teams in schools to start ventures of their own. This is a natural field for partnership since companies have so much to offer – ideas, materials, advisers and above all encouragement.

I have concentrated on business's approach to the partnership, because that is where my experience lies. I would however expect the schools to have equally firm objectives and to look to business for the answers to such questions as, what skills do you require now and in the future and what do you expect of us? These are proper questions to ask and we have not made much of a fist of answering them in the past, even accepting the difficulty of answering them at all. The major difficulty we face in trying to predict our demands on the educational system is the rate of change, especially technological change. This point underlines the importance we place on the ability and willingness to learn. Managing change demands a sound educational base in mathematics and in the use of language – to understand and convey ideas – and the capacity to add on to that base the skills which a rapidly changing business world will require. Flexibility is what we try to build in to all our company systems and flexibility of mind is what will be needed to run them. This is the best answer to the concern about business having a narrow vocational approach to education; it would not be in our own interests, since the specific vocational skills we are looking for today will be obsolescent in five years time.

The point on which I would like to end is that companies are educational institutions. This provides a firm basis for the partnership between business and schools. Companies invest money and management effort in training and I believe that the companies which give the highest priority to that investment are those which are most likely to compete successfully. While our training effort is mainly directed to meeting the needs of the business, some courses such as those which introduce people to the use of computers have broader implications. Above all, this investment in training encourages people to recognise that they can continue to learn throughout their lives, through the institutions for open learning, which have followed the pioneering lead of the Open University, and through the possibilities which video and distance learning open up. All of these have an essential part to play in the promotion of continuing education.

It has always seemed extraordinary and absurd that the conventional view of education should have been that it stopped on leaving school or college: extraordinary because it meant that learning was considered separately from experience, when the two should nourish each other; absurd because it implied that a single dose of education at the outset could inoculate us for the rest of our lives – that can never have made much sense and it certainly does not now, in a technological world. The concern we all share, however, is that too many children leave school at the earliest opportunity with no desire to continue studies of any kind. The common aims on which we can build the partnership we are looking for are to provide jointly a better bridge between schools and companies and to encourage their pupils, when they become *our* employees, to take advantage of the opportunities to continue learning throughout their lives.

[8]

Redesigning the wheel: technology education for a sustainable society

GARY BENENSON

Treat the Earth well
It was not given to you by your parents
It was loaned to you by your children
Kenyan proverb

I INTRODUCTION: THE AMBIGUOUS CHALLENGE

In talking of *the* challenge to education, this book has largely been talking about technology. This implies that there is general agreement on the nature of the challenge faced by education. I would argue that this is not so. On the contrary, there are very divergent views, based on conflicting beliefs about the relationships between technology, nature, society and culture in the modern world.

The dominant idea in the industrialised world is that economic growth, usually defined by GNP, and the accelerated development of technology are of unquestioned value. This position is variously described as one based on 'economic values' by Pacey (1983), as the 'Western Worldview' by Clark (1989), and as the 'individualistic political culture' by Schwarz and Thompson (1990). According to this view, nature is ultimately forgiving of human transgression, 'a technological fix exists for every human problem' (Clark 1989: 295), and the proper role of society is to offer the least possible resistance to human enterprise and ingenuity.

An alternative view draws heavily on an egalitarian vision of society, combined with deep concern over the environmental impacts of modern technology. Pacey (1983) describes this belief system as one based on 'user or need values', while Schwarz and Thompson (1990) refer to it as the 'egalitarian political culture'. Clark (1989) calls for a new worldview, based on the prescript that 'life is not to be lived in isolation, either from Nature or from one another' (p. 328). Advocates of this position argue that growth-oriented economics and the technological imperative are responsible for wide inequity, social conflict and environmental degradation.

In its own way, each viewpoint perceives serious problems today and serious concerns for the future. Advocates of the growth-oriented position, such as National Research Council (1985), are concerned with the growing gap between the quantity and quality of the technical workforce on the one hand, and the needs of industry and the military on the other. Adherents of an alternative worldview, such as Clark (1989), Commoner (1990) and the World Commission on Environment and Development (1987) see a very different kind of gap. They maintain that rapid developments in technology have far surpassed the capacity of society or the environment to keep pace. While the former group warns of threats to national competitiveness and general economic growth (National Science Foundation 1987), the latter questions the ability of our culture to survive without rethinking its use of technology.

The nature of the challenge to education depends on how one views these basic issues. This chapter is based on the idea that the environmental and social concerns expressed above are real and very urgent. I see several interrelated challenges which demand immediate attention from our educational institutions:

- Maintenance of the earth's life-support system requires a fundamental redesign of the 'technosphere' – the objects created by humans.
- Rapid developments in technology have left behind a strong sense of alienation, powerlessness and cynicism among the general public. Most people have a very limited understanding of the world they live in, and little voice in the decisions which will shape its future.
- Technological change and economic growth have bypassed or even displaced large sectors in our society, particularly poor and working-class Blacks and Hispanics. Disparities in the educational system both reflect and contribute to the problem.
- Public education at all levels is under attack. Many institutions have undergone budget cuts which compromise their basic viability.

Each of these points has been made before, but often in isolation from the others. This chapter suggests a unified way of looking at them. The next section asks the question: what is the appropriate role of technical people in society? To what extent can they be part of the solutions to the challenges outlined above? In the following section, the focus shifts to technology education: what ought to be its aims and methods? Section 4 explores some of the current movements in education, and measures them against the conclusions of the previous section. In section 5, I describe some of my own efforts to develop new approaches in technology education. Section 6 concludes with some thoughts about the future of urban public education.

2 TECHNOLOGISTS RETHINKING TECHNOLOGY

The Gulf war (1990–1) should remind us of the fragile foundations beneath our technological superstructure. Dependence on oil fouls the air and water of our planet, leads periodically to economic chaos, and precipitates international conflict. Nevertheless, few in our society raise basic questions about the long-term future of modern technology.

Until recently, many found it convenient to dismiss environmentalism as misguided or even self-serving. McPhee (1971), for example quotes a resort developer who states that conservationists 'worship trees and sacrifice human beings to those trees. They want to save the things that they like, all for themselves' (p. 95). Within the past few years, however, concern over the environmental effects of technology has become widespread. Indeed, these concerns have surfaced in some unexpected places: the Boston University Business School (Post 1990), the pro-military wing of the US Senate (Shabecoff 1990), and even the Nuclear Weapons Program of the United States Department of Energy (Schneider 1990), not to mention the advertising campaigns of a myriad of industrial corporations.

Some still maintain that economic and environmental concerns are mutually exclusive. For Wenk (1989) the fundamental conflict is between short – and long-term goals: should present satisfactions be sacrificed in favour of the well-being of future generations? Ecology says yes, while economics says no (p. 149). However, a growing trend of thought describes many situations in which economic and environmental objectives can be achieved simultaneously. Conservation of non-renewable energy and material resources are only the most obvious examples. Conservation makes sense whether one is concerned about pollution, energy independence, national or international security, the cost of living, economic growth, uncertain but plausible climate catastrophes, or international competitiveness (Schneider 1989: 267). As a native and current New Yorker, my own favourite example concerns the New York City Subway System. Reducing or eliminating the fare would increase the number of passengers, decrease automobile traffic and travel time, make the trains safer, reduce poverty and unemploy-ment by making it easier for people to get to work, and measurably improve the air quality.

The apparent conflict between economic productivity and environ-mental quality is dealt with in detail by Commoner (1990), who argues that the long-run interests even of large corporations are served by environmentally sound policies. The costs to society of existing pollution are staggering, in the form of increased medical expenses, building maintenance, nuclear and toxic waste clean-ups. The costs associated with global climate change are likely to be even greater (Passell 1989). The proper evaluation of technology requires far more than narrow technical knowledge, or simplistic bottom-line accounting. Pacey (1983) develops the concept of 'innovative dialogue' as a mechanism for 'balan-cing narrow specialist views against broader insights' (p. 159). Schwarz and Thompson (1990) make a similar point in much greater detail. They promote the concept of 'constructive technology assessment', which transcends the conflict between the egalitarian and individualistic politi-cal cultures. It is possible, they maintain, to develop 'selection rules' which provide specific guidelines for integrating technical and social criteria in decision making.

Some have actually used the tools of technology to analyse the limi-tations and contradictions associated with our technological society. A systems engineer predicts that human society will enter a de-industrial phase within the next century, due to the exhaustion of natural resources. His argument is based on the lack of sufficient feedback from the environmental system to the social system (Duncan 1989). A mathematician turned economist bases a similar prediction on the laws of thermodynamics. To the well-known four laws, he adds a fifth law which is parallel to the second: like energy resources, material resources become less available as they are used, due to inevitable processes of wear and decay (Pacey 1983: 63). A physicist uses the basic mathematics of exponential growth to refute the statements of a wide variety of experts on the energy crisis (Bartlett 1978). His article, which is directed at high school and college teachers, concludes with the statement, 'We must emphasise to our students that they have a very special role in our society, a role that follows directly from their analytical abilities. It is their responsibility (and ours) to become the great humanists' (p. 887).

Nevertheless, many technologists remain unconvinced of the import-ance of environmental and social issues. A recent special issue of *Spectrum* (Institute of Electrical and Electronics Engineers 1989), is entitled *The*

Threat of Peace. Unfortunately, no irony is intended. The magazine provides engineers with information, anecdotes and advice about how to deal with the effects of the US military budget cuts. There is no suggestion that there might be a positive side to the decrease in world tensions. Yet the transition to a more sustainable society will require a great deal of technical expertise, much of which could come from declining arms industries. The Eureka research consortium, sponsored by nineteen European countries, is funding the development of new environmentally sound technologies. Many of the firms involved are former armaments manufacturers seeking new markets (Clery 1990).

A new kind of technical professional will be needed to design and implement socially and environmentally responsible technologies. In the 1940s, a group of British doctors founded the new field of social medicine, in order to respond to people's mental and physical needs 'beyond the conventional boundaries of medical science' (Pacey 1983: 52). What would it take to found a new field called 'social technology'?

3 TECHNOLOGY EDUCATION: FACING THE FUTURE

Many studies have appeared which catalogue the sorry state of science and technology education and awareness among children and adults. Recent examples include the American Association for the Advancement of Science (1989), Science Council of Canada (1984) and the Royal Society of Great Britain, cited in Birke (1990). In all three countries, the reports describe a familiar vicious cycle: fewer science teachers with poorer preparation are producing fewer science and technical graduates, leading to further reductions in the number and quality of the teaching force. Presently used materials, curricula and instructional methods often fail to achieve their stated objectives: 'They emphasise the learning of answers more than the exploration of questions, memory at the expense of critical thought, bits and pieces of information instead of understandings in context, recitation instead of argument, reading instead of doing' (American Association for the Advancement of Science 1989: 14). There is little if anything in the curriculum to excite the vast majority of students about science and technology, even though the artifacts of technology pervade their everyday lives.

Among female and urban minority students, the situation is considerably worse. Starting about age 9, girls show less interest and achievement in science than boys, and this trend continues through adulthood (Rosser 1990: 56). A similar pattern affects urban Black and Hispanic students in relation to whites (Cheek 1989a: 75). Compounding these problems are the draconian budget cuts which affect public education institutions at all levels. The virtual exclusion of women, Blacks and Hispanics from science and technology education is tragic in several respects. Educational inequity, particularly in a highly technological society, contradicts the principles of democracy and strengthens the existence of a dual society. It removes valuable talent from the workforce. It contributes to social alienation, conflict and violence. The fields of science and technology must provide greater access to traditionally excluded groups.

This last point has been made frequently, but another needs to be added. The most harmful effects of technology and the need for rational, informed decision making are most obvious in large urban centres. Who will make the decisions regarding the future of cities, and on what basis? It is insufficient to attract urban students simply to learn technology as it is now practised. Urban educational institutions should attempt to lay the basis for the new 'social technology', by developing both a new kind of professional, as well as a technically aware citizenry. Only then will it become possible for people to make informed choices about the uses of technology in their communities.

To achieve these goals, dramatic changes are urgently needed in the conduct of science and technology education. At the present time, most students find these subjects to be difficult, boring, abstract, and irrelevant to the problems and experiences of their lives. In order to engage them in thinking creatively about technology, three ingredients are essential. Technology education must become inquiry-based (interactive) interdisciplinary and socially relevant.

The inquiry approach calls for the active participation of the student in planning and carrying out scientific investigations (Harlen 1985). Inquiry-based learning has taken root in elementary science education, particularly in the UK, but inquiry approaches are largely untested above the middle-school level, or in technology education generally. Beginning with the sobering insight that 'learning is not necessarily an outcome of teaching' (p. 145), the AAAS (1989) develops a strong case for inquiry-based learning. Students need opportunities to become acquainted with their immediate environment; develop questions about the things that they see, taste, hear and touch; make systematic observations and measurements; develop their own interpretations of what the evidence means; share the responsibility for learning with others; learn effective ways of documenting and presenting their findings; and learn to question accepted beliefs, including those presented by the teacher.

Technology education needs to become interdisciplinary, because technology itself is interdisciplinary. Technologies often fail to meet their objectives because of narrow thinking which ignores the social, cultural and environmental contexts of production, maintenance and use. For example, public schools are frequently unable to use perfectly functioning computers for purely organisational reasons: lack of supplies, hardware or software incompatibilities, insufficient staff development. Many students sense that something crucial is missing from the conventional textbook/lecture/examination approach to technical education. A purely technical treatment is at odds with the real world. Pacey (1983) recalls, 'the textbooks from which I was supposed to learn soil mechanics discussed the design of embankments, dams, foundations and highways almost entirely without giving examples of real highways or dams, so questions of context and socio-economic background could never arise' (p. 166).

Social relevance is the third essential ingredient in technology education: 'A strong argument for convincing females that they should become scientists is that they can have more direct influence over policies and decisions controlling the uses of technology' (Rosser 1990: 61). This argument fails, of course, if the topics of study are foreign to the students' actual experiences and concerns. This point is made graphically by Unks (1984), who observes that 'The urban curriculum – even at its best – has usually worn a pair of bib overalls. Its shape resembles the barn, the chicken coop and the silo more than the museum, the traffic jam or the skyscraper' (p. 443). The solution is obvious: 'Issues such as solid waste management, chemical pollution of the air and water, urban health problems, changing workplace quality and declining industrial jobs, high-rise housing, noise pollution and crowding . . . all bear on urban youth' (Waks 1989: 27). Technology education must concern itself with the impact of technology on the students' own lives, cultures, hopes and fears. Raywid (1987) makes the point in a secondary school context: 'If we are serious about wanting to keep prospective dropouts in school, then clearly what we must do is change the way they feel about school. They have to be convinced that education is of value, that it is worthwhile and can make a difference in their lives.'

4 SHAKING THE SLUMBERING GIANT

Professor John Truxal, feedback control expert and Co-director of the New Liberal Arts (NLA) programme (see below), has described educational institutions as 'homeostatic'. His point is well taken. The resistance to change in schools and universities is remarkable, given their role in the development of ideas. However, Professor Truxal's own work contradicts his claim. The NLA programme, and the related movement for Science Technology and Society (STS) studies, represent significant initiatives for change at the college level.

Cheek (1989b) reviews twelve major high-school STS curricula from the US and the UK. Included are efforts by the Biological Sciences Study Committee (BSCS), American Chemical Society (ACS), the Association for Science Education of the UK, and the Washington, DC, public schools. Review criteria included the extent to which the curricula 'help students understand that they are interdependent members of an urban society' and demonstrate how informed individuals 'can make a positive contribution to the urban environment'. He concludes that 'none of the materials surveyed contains sufficient quality and coverage of these guideline principles to be used "as is" in urban schools with large minority student populations'. On the other hand, nearly all of them had 'some material that would be of use to further curriculum development efforts' (p. 306).

Cheek's assessment could easily be applied to college-level programmes as well. The New Liberal Arts (NLA) programme of the Alfred P. Sloam Foundation was founded in 1982. Its objective is to provide liberal-arts students with meaningful experiences in quantitative reasoning and the applications of technology in a wide range of fields. Courses related to the NLA programme have been developed in such fields as art, psychology, economics, law, music, history, philosophy and public policy, as well as engineering and the natural sciences (Truxal and Visich, undated). Although it is difficult to summarise such a wide variety of activities, one salient feature of the NLA is its concentration in small private colleges and elite universities. The NLA curricula are strongly interdisciplinary and many are interactive, providing a hands-on introduction to technology. However, they are generally lacking in social relevance, particularly to urban audiences.

Interdisciplinary STS programmes were developed in response to many of the issues raised in this paper.

They attempt to provide socially relevant, interdisciplinary learning. Major topics of study include environmental issues, the history and philosophy of technology and, increasingly, gender issues. Many STS course outlines are presented in Reynolds (1987) and Rothschild (1988). Some of these course offerings are concentrated in specialised STS departments, while others are listed under one or more traditional disciplines. STS courses tend to have a global or national focus, rather than an urban or local one. Few of these courses provide substantial technical content, and even fewer offer hands-on experiences with technology. An innovative exception is the HumEn programme at the Colorado School of Mines (Olds and Miller, 1990).

Notwithstanding their limitations, STS and NLA curricula represent seminal efforts to provide broader contexts for the study of technology. They have affected many institutions, and go part of the way towards meeting the challenges outlined in previous sections. STS and NLA must be the starting points for any future initiatives to develop interactive, interdisciplinary, socially relevant learning experiences.

5 TOWARDS AN URBAN FOCUS FOR STS

As noted above, the vast majority of STS activities are neither focused on urban problems, nor oriented towards urban audiences. The studies by Waks (1989), Cheek (1989b), and others from the same US Department of education report confirm this point, and suggest remedies for change. Unfortunately, there have been few concrete outcomes from this excellent project, which involved university researchers in education, the natural and social sciences, and black studies; administrators from five large city school systems; and science teachers from inner-city high schools.

In this section, I describe my own very preliminary efforts at the City College to implement the goals outlined by Waks (1989) and Cheek (1989a). Perhaps these tentative and fragmentary experiences will inspire others to do better.

Communication, film and video 241: technology and communications.
The Department of Communications, Film and Video (CFV) prepares its students for careers in electronic and print journalism, and other media-industry occupations. Approximately half of the students were born in Asia, Africa, Latin America or the Caribbean. As future media professionals, CFV students will thus be in a unique position to understand issues of international development and to communicate about them to diverse audiences in this country. However, their education is severely lacking in the areas of science and technology. Thus, they are poorly equipped to understand, interpret or communicate about the myriad of public-policy issues which have a technical basis.

In an effort to remedy this defect, and to test some of the ideas outlined above, an existing course called technology of communications was revised to include a major component on 'Communicating about Technology'. The course revisions were supported by a grant from the

City College President's Fund for Innovation and Excellence; and the newly redesigned course was team-taught with Professor Mark Schulman, then Chairman of the CFV Department. The new component on 'Communicating about Technology' consisted of an introductory section on the scientific method, followed by two case studies of public issues about which there are serious disagreements among technical experts.

To gain some understanding of how scientists draw inferences about cause and effect, students were first asked to perform three simple 'kitchen experiments in atmospheric science'. These experiences were intended to convince them that scientific theories are the product of logical reasoning about real experiences. The students performed the experiments with great enthusiasm and creativity. Each experiment had a counter-intuitive result, related to the existence of water vapour in the atmosphere. In the ensuing discussion, students were encouraged to develop a chain of reasoning leading from their own experimental results to an inference about the existence and nature of atmospheric water vapour.

Before doing the public-policy case studies, we held a discussion about the consequences for democratic decision making of widespread scientific and technical ignorance. Although it was generally agreed that the public ought to know more about science and technology, there was disagreement about the origins of the problem. Some blamed the lay public for not making a greater effort; while others felt that scientists and/or policy makers were at fault for deliberately restricting the flow of information or for presenting the issues in an obscure manner.

The case studies were based upon two controversial current issues which involve science and technology:

- the so-called 'greenhouse effect', and the reported global warming trend;
- the Strategic Defense Initiative (SDI), popularly known as 'Star Wars'.

In each instance, students were exposed to sharply divergent journalistic accounts, both in written and video form. Class time was spent analysing these materials for their underlying assumptions, and ideological contexts, as well as for technical content.

Very few of the students began this course with any substantial background in science or technology. There was a strong tendency to reject any sort of technical discussion as too difficult or obscure. The experiments drew them in, because the results were unexpected, and required some kind of explanation. The case studies provided a different kind of motivation for understanding technology. Students became convinced that these were important issues which might affect their own futures. They also became aware that some technical background was a necessity for understanding the articles and videos. Ultimately, however, many of them realised that much of the controversy, though couched in technical language, was actually about economic, political, social or cultural interests and values.

Electromechanical devices and systems (technology 462)

The technical aspects of the course covered programmable logic controllers, robotics and process control technologies. I developed laboratory experiments in the first two of these areas, and built the classroom discussion and assignments around the lab experiences. During the final third of the course, I used automotive electronic emission control systems to illustrate process-control technologies. Meanwhile, the laboratory work consisted of collaborative design projects based upon the earlier experiments. Students were overwhelmingly enthusiastic about the course, because it gave them group experiences in conceiving, designing, implementing and documenting real systems.

Midway through the course, I asked the class to express arguments for or against a statement: 'Industrial automation is a benefit to society.' As a way of stimulating discussion, I wrote their positions on the blackboard under the headings 'Pro' and 'Con'. For each argument offered by a student, I made a counter-argument, which I wrote in the opposite column. By the end of the discussion, the blackboard resembled Table 8.1.

Table 8.1 Industrial automation is a benefit to society?

Pro	Con
Makes some jobs safer, by removing workers from hazardous environments	Makes some jobs more dangerous, by replacing human judgment with pre-programmed algorithmic procedures
Lowers the cost of a product, making it more available to consumers	Leads to unemployment, and therefore less money in the economy
Makes work more interesting, because more technical knowledge is needed	Makes work less interesting, because craft skills are eliminated
Leads to higher quality products, because of more accurate control over production parameters	Leads to a lower quality product, because machines cannot respond as well as humans to subtle changes in materials and conditions

In the course of this exercise, it became clear that each of these arguments might have more validity for some forms of automation than for
others. For example, robotic technologies are frequently used to handle
materials in the course of hazardous operations, such as spray painting
or welding. On the other hand, the argument about the removal of
human judgement has been made in connection with numerical control
technologies (Noble 1984: 245–6 and 345).

During the portion of the course on automotive emission controls,
the discussion of social issues was less focused, but more sustained. We
examined in technical detail how process-control technologies are used
to control emissions and improve fuel efficiency. At the same time, we
also looked at societal solutions to the emission problem, such as
enforced car pooling, improved mass transit, 'car-less days', and legally
mandated conversion to less polluting engines.

Many students tended to take starkly moralistic or fatalistic viewpoints about the prospects of any satisfactory resolution. More than
once, a statement to the effect that 'people are just going to have to
stop driving their cars' was rejoined by the the comment that 'they're
just not going to do it; their car is too important to them'. I found it
difficult to convey the idea that people's views on technology are neither
innate nor inevitable, but rather a product of a particular culture at a
particular time in history. For example, except for some Asian students,
no one was prepared to believe that there are nearly twice as many
bicycles as cars in use in the world today.

During the class meeting immediately after the one on the social
effects of automation, I asked the students whether that discussion had
been worthwhile, and whether or not it really belonged in the course.
One student responded that 'students at Columbia or NYU might have
time for that kind of discussion, but here at City College, all we're
interested in is finding jobs'. He was rejoined by a student who said,
'We all want jobs, sure, but we also have to be concerned with the
environment, because we'll have to live in it.' Another expressed the
opinion that 'nobody is interested in the long term, but we should be',
and then used the example of asbestos in college buildings as an object
of his concern. A fourth student commented, 'Just in order to do the
job, we'll need to see the total picture.'

At the very end of the course, there was a student-led evaluation of
all its major aspects. The introduction of social issues into the course
was a major topic during the evaluation. I asked the class a question
which the Dean of Engineering had asked me: '*Did they feel that the
introduction of social issues had replaced technical material which should have been*

covered?' The responses fell into two camps. Several students said that the effect of technology on society was an important topic, but that it did not belong in a required course called electromechanical devices. It should be offered as a separate, elective course instead. Others disagreed, saying that the material was indeed part of the subject material of the course, and reflected a 'deep approach, which sees everything as related'. One student said that the course had 'opened our eye to how technology will affect the environment, and ultimately, us'.

In order to gain some insight into how the course had changed the students' view on technical education, I took an informal survey. I asked, first, how many students would take a course on technology and society, if it were offered as an elective. Ten out of twenty students raised their hands. Then I asked how many of those who said yes would have had the same answer had they never taken my course, or any other which introduced social issues into the technical curriculum. This time, only three students answered affirmatively. This bit of informal research strongly suggests that most students would not normally choose to take an interdisciplinary course on their own initiative; but that *they might be stimulated to do so* if such material was first incorporated into a technical course.

The physics of energy conservation in architecture (architecture 410.4: independent study)

This course was developed in response to a request by five sophomore-level Architecture students, all women. They asked me to offer an independent study course in physics, with relevance to their major, in lieu of the required general physics course. I agreed to do so without pay, in exchange for their willingness to participate in an experiment in socially relevant, interactive education.

The students and I then developed an outline for a course on energy conservation in buildings, a topic which does not appear in the regular curriculum. The first day of the term, I led a discussion of the global energy problem. Because three of the five students had been born in the Caribbean, I asked them to consider some of the differences between tropical and modern architecture. They recalled from their own experiences that buildings in the tropics remain much cooler than modern buildings, without the use of air conditioning. I also reviewed some of the facts concerning energy use in buildings. 'As much energy leaks through American windows every year as flows through the Alaska pipeline' (Flavin and Durning 1988: 18). During the course of the term, the global energy problem provided the context for the more technical aspects of the course.

We met once a week to discuss the principles of thermodynamics, heat transfer and climate as they affect building design. Working as a group, the students then devised and performed their own experiments to explore physical phenomena. I frequently suggested ways to modify or extend their investigations, and provided some insight on the meaning of their data. But the overall design, implementation and quantitative interpretation remained their responsibility.

During the course, the students designed and performed three major experiments. The first dealt with the law of conservation of energy. Using a microwave oven, they studied the rates of temperature increase when similar quantities of energy were delivered to different volumes of water. The second experiment involved both Newton's law of cooling, and the relative insulating capabilities of styrofoam and glass. After heating a standard volume of water in closed glass and styrofoam containers, they removed the heating element, and recorded the cooling curves. The final experiment concerned passive solar heating. They constructed cardboard cartons with plastic 'windows', and used them to measure the amount of heat energy which could be obtained from direct solar radiation. At the end of the course, I asked the students to write a collaborative final paper expressing what they had learned in the course and its relevance for them as future architects.

The course was least successful in accomplishing its technical objectives. The students were frequently unable to perform the calculations and analyse the data from their experiments – although each had passed the math prerequisite. It was clear that they had never been required to apply quantitative reasoning to the analysis of real data. We felt that much more time should have been spent in addressing problem-solving and data-analysis techniques.

At the same time, their investigations were very revealing to them about the nature of science. At first, they felt very frustrated and disoriented, and several considered dropping the course. 'This is not like any science course,' they told me. 'Science has definite answers. These experiments have no beginning and no end.' However, soon their views of science began to change. They found it very exciting to be able to design their own experiments, and pursue their own questions and ideas. They also appreciated the collaborative learning style, and frequently emphasised that none of them could have achieved individually what they had achieved as a group.

In the students' view, the most positive aspect of the course was that it had brought them 'closer to the real world'. It had made them aware of the energy problem, and given them a desire to incorporate the principles of energy conservation and climate-sensitive design in their own future work. They saw the importance of understanding difficult principles of thermodynamics and heat transfer, and felt motivated to learn more science. At the same time, they felt that modern architecture should not ignore the experiences of indigenous people. They wrote, 'The technologies of indigenous people must be incorporated with the advances in energy conservation for maximum human comfort and efficiency.' I felt that the course was very successful in raising their environmental, social and technical awareness.

6 CONCLUSION: A PROCESS OF RECUPERATION IN PUBLIC EDUCATION

This paper has tried to establish that interactive, interdisciplinary, socially relevant education can indeed address the major challenges outlined in the introduction. Some examples were provided in the previous section to indicate the shape such education might take. They suggest that it is possible to accomplish the following goals:

- Make students aware and concerned about problems of the global and local environment.
- Alter their sense that they can never understand nor affect the uses of technology.
- Motivate Black, Hispanic and female students to study technology, based on its relevance to their own lives.

Unfortunately, it is doubtful whether any of these objectives can be attained in the face of mounting threats to the integrity of public education. Without adequate or even minimal funding, educational institutions are forced into a reactive, defensive posture, from which little innovation can come forth. Education can hardly meet any new challenges if it can barely meet its payroll.

On the other hand, new thinking in one area sometimes stimulates new thinking in another. The educational changes proposed here could also form the basis for a different kind of effort to restore adequate funding. The public has a vital stake in our success in meeting the challenges to education. 'What the future holds in store for individual human beings, the nation and the world depends largely on the wisdom with which humans use science and technology. But that, in turn, depends on the character, distribution and effectiveness of the education that people receive' (American Association for the Advancement of

Science 1989: 12). This statement is especially true in large urban areas, where the future seems least hopeful. Educators and educational leaders ought to make this appeal directly to the public, over the heads of the politicians.

References

American Association for the Advancement of Science (1989), *Science for All Americans: a project 2061 report on literacy goals in science. mathematics and technology*, Washington, DC, AAAS.

Bartlett, Albert (1978), 'Forgotten fundamentals of the energy crisis', *AM. J. Phys*, September 46(9), p. 876–88.

Birke, Lynda (1990), 'Selling science to the public, *New Scientist*, 18 August, 1730, pp. 40–4.

Cheek, Dennis (1989a), 'Science education for urban minority students – current problems and potential solutions', *Technological Literacy for the 'New Majority': enhancing secondary science education through science/technology/society (STS) for urban/minority youth*, (ERIC 310–987), Washington, DC, US Department of Education, pp. 71–125.

Cheek, Dennis (1989b), 'Review of major high school level STS curricula in light of the project guidelines for STS education for urban and minority students', *Technological Literacy for the 'New Majority': enhancing secondary science education through Science/Technology/Society (STS) for Urban/Minority Youth*, (ERIC 310–987), Washington, DC: US Department of Education, pp. 253–308.

Clark, Mary (1989), *Ariadne's Thread: the search for new modes of meaning*, New York, St Martin's Press.

Clery, Daniel (1990), 'The greening of Eureka', *New Scientist, 9 June, 126* (1720), p.38.

Commoner, Barry (1990), *Making Peace with the Planet*, New York, Pantheon Books.

Duncan, Richard (1989), 'Evolution, technology and the natural environment', *Proceedings of the St Lawrence Section Annual Meeting of the American Society for Engineering Education*, Binghamton, NY, p. 14B1–11 – 14B1–20.

Flavin, Christopher and Durning, Alan (1988), *Building on Success: the age of energy efficiency*, Worldwatch Paper 82, Washington, DC, Worldwatch Institute.

Harlen, Wynne (ed.), (1985), *Primary Science . . . Taking the Plunge: how to teach primary science more effectively*, Oxford, Heinemann Educational Books.

Institute of Electrical and Electronics Engineers (1989), *Special Report: the threat of peace, Spectrum*, November, 26(11).

McPhee, John (1971), *Encounters with the Archdruid (Narratives about a Conservationist and Three of his Natural Enemies*, New York, Farrar, Straus & Giroux.

National Research Council (1985), *Engineering Education and Practice in the United States: foundations of our techno-economic future*, Washington, DC, National Academy Press.

National Science Foundation (1987). *Human Talent for Competitiveness* (NSF 87–24), Washington, DC, NSF.

Noble, David F. (1984), *Forces of Production*, New York, Alfred Knopf Publishing Co.

Olds, Barbara and Miller, Jonathan (1990), 'Meaningful humanities studies for engineering students: a new approach', *1990 ASEE Annual Conference Proceedings*, Washington: ASEE, p. 1040–2.

Pacey, Arnold (1983), *The Culture of Technology*, Cambridge, Mass., MIT Press.

Passell, Peter (1989), 'Staggering cost is foreseen to curb warming of earth', *New York Times*, 19 November, p. A1.

Post, James E. (1990), 'The greening of management', *Issues in Science and Technology*, Summer, 6(4), pp. 68–72.

Raywid, Mary Anne (1987), 'Making school work for the new majority', *Journal of Negro Education*, 56(2), pp. 221–7, (quoted in Waks 1989).

Reynolds, Terry, (ed.) (1987), *The Machine in the University: sample course syllabi for the history of technology and technology studies*, (2nd edn.), Bethlehem, PA: Lehigh University.

Rosser, Sue V. (1990). *Female-Friendly Science*, New York, Pergamon Press.

Rothschild, Joan (1988), *Teaching Technology from a Feminist Perspective: a practical guide*, New York, Pergamon Press.

Schneider, Keith (1990), 'New mission at energy dept. bomb makers turn to cleanup', *New York Times*, 17 August, p. A1.

Schneider, Stephen (1989), *Global Warming: are we entering the greenhouse century?*, San Francisco, Sierra Club Books.

Schwarz, Michiel and Thompson, Michael (1990), *Divided We Stand: redefining politics, technology and social choice*, Philadelphia, University of Pennsylvania Press.

Science Council of Canada (1984), *Science for Every Student: educating Canadians for tomorrow's world*, (Report 36), Ottawa, SCC.

Shabecoff, Philip (1990), 'Senator urges military resources be turned to environmental battle', *New York Times*, 29 June, p. A1.

Truxal, John and Visich, Marian, (eds) (undated), *The New Liberal Arts: Educational Examples*, Stony Brook, NY, SUNY Stony Brook Department of Technology and Society.

Unks, Gerald (1984), 'The new demography: implications for the school curriculum', *Education in Urban Society*, 16, p. 443–62, (quoted from Cheek 1989a).

Waks, Leonard (1989), 'Science through science/technology/society (STS) for urban minority youth', *Technological Literacy for the 'New Majority': enhancing secondary science education through science/technology/society (STS) for urban/minority youth* (ERIC 310–987), Washington, DC: US Department of Education, pp. 12–31.

Wenk, Edward (1989), *Tradeoffs: imperatives of choice in a high-tech world*, Baltimore, MD, Johns Hopkins University Press.

World Commission on Environment and Development (1987), *Our Common Future*, New York, Oxford University Press.

[9]

Using telecommunications to enhance educational experiences

SHEILA O. GERSH AND ALFRED S. POSAMENTIER

INTRODUCTION

Although the computer has come to dominate the ways in which Americans conduct their daily lives – from making telephone calls to depositing money in bank accounts – it has yet to become an equally dominant tool in the conduct of the American classroom. The key reasons for this chasm between the growing technological applications of industry and the continuing chalk-and-eraser dependency of the classroom may be attributed to the lack of funds for equipment, a dearth of properly trained educators, and the unavailability of software that can easily be integrated into the current school curriculum (Barbour 1987; McCarthy 1988).

In fact, both education and industry may be held responsible for neglecting the utilisation of technology as a component of classroom life. For example, industry has developed software often without sufficient consultation between program developers and current educational practitioners. The resulting product frequently focuses on the glitz of presentation rather than on the substance of curriculum and classroom needs, thus relegating the computer to novelty status. On the other hand, educators, many of whom have never been exposed to computers, have been both fearful of the technology and reluctant to take the time to learn to use the computer as an instructional tool, mistrustful that it can enhance teaching and learning in a dynamic interactive mode.

However, there is a growing number of educators and industry representatives who are searching together to identify more meaningful and significant roles for the computer in the current school curriculum, seeking not one ideal but a portfolio of strategies for the improvement of instruction through technology. Numerous experiments involving the use of the computer in various subjects have produced some exciting innovations, but there is a need to emphasise the role of the computer as an integral part of the classroom, furthering not only subject mastery but the processes of thinking and inquiry. Towards this end, we have sought to use and explore the technological advances made in telecommunications to enhance pre-college learning experiences. It is our contention that when we harness the technology to enable students to ask questions, find relevant and non-trivial information, gather data, analyse trends and make predictions, the computer becomes a worthwhile educational tool (White 1989).

For the past decade schools have been making investments in computers for classroom use. Early uses of computers were largely limited to electronic workbooks with drill and practice exercises, tutorials, simulations, and number/word games (Bozeman and House 1988). While educators have been dealing with the question of whether or not to use computers in the classroom, little or no effort has been made to use the computer to change the ways in which students learn. Pearlman (1989) and McCarthy (1988) have reported that computers are still not universally integrated into the curriculum. In addition, they found that only 15 per cent of all teachers in the United States actually use computers in their teaching. 'Computers are failing as teaching aids' (Pearlman 1989) and 'as computers are currently utilised, they have little or no impact on student achievement'. According to Pearlman (1989), it is possible to put millions of computers in the schools without producing any real change in education. In other words, there are major differences of approach that have to be put into effect if computers are to function as enhancements to learning rather than as the classroom equivalents of Nintendo.

We believe that when used correctly, computers can improve student achievement, have a positive impact on school climate and change the way students learn. Computers can be used to help educators move away from a didactic learning mode to a collaborative one, developing new and exciting roles for both teachers and students in the process. When students are treated as active workers, the expertise of teachers becomes ever more critical in facilitating student learning (McCarthy 1988). The teacher moves from being the dominant purveyor of information to the enabler of learning, encouraging the development of divergent thinking and problem solving.

To make these instructional changes possible, however, teachers must become sophisticated consumers of technology and become cognisant of the expanded capabilities afforded the learning scene by technological advances. With this knowledge teachers can assume greater responsibility and authority for decisions about the kind of technology that most appropriately supports their expanded role as well as the curriculum and the instructional needs of their students.

It is true that the 1980s saw a significant increase in the uses of telecommunications and personal computers to deliver instruction (Sigliano, Joslyn, and Levin 1989). As we have stated, however, educators have not yet fully exploited the potential of technology as a dynamic learning tool integrated into the essence of the learning experience. The computer's use in word processing and accessing electronic databases may be a chief function of the computer to enable students in the traditional classroom to become part of a global classroom. According to Tinker (1989), students who are able to access information electronically could be learning vastly more in the right instructional setting equipped with the right tools.

TECHNOLOGY APPLICATION: TELECOMMUNICATIONS

Telecommunications is one example of the power of technology to provide a more stimulating instructional setting. Information, translated into electronic signals, is sent via telephone cables, and/or by satellite to worldwide destinations between two computers. These 'electronic mailboxes' function much the same way as ordinary mail is moved between mailboxes. Naturally, the time involved in electronic mail is nearly instantaneous and the cost is relatively low. In education, telecommunications is generally used to enable students to communicate with counterparts locally, nationally, or internationally and to access remote data bases. In practice, sometimes these two uses are combined.

Telecommunications can make learning and instruction more exciting and important, broadening students' perspectives as well as motivating and exciting them about lessons that may have grown routine. Students are more willing to get involved in recreational reading and writing when it is done for 'real' audiences in far away places. As an integral part of the curriculum, telecommunications does not have to be something 'in addition' to what teachers are already charged to teach. According to Mageau (1990), it also promotes professional growth for teachers while it helps encourage the development of research skills amongst students (Schrum 1988). Perhaps most importantly telecommunications adds interest and enthusiasm to the curriculum, while providing students with a better understanding of other cultures and world events.

Although this technology is (relatively speaking) in its infancy, it is moving at a rapid pace. Teachers are beginning to use telecommunications through a variety of networks allowing for the creation of databases and on-line projects. They are developing curriculum materials which not only facilitate use of this technology, but as a by-product integrate heretofore unrelated topics in the curriculum. Most often these projects are teacher initiated and supported. There are numerous national/international projects, using and exploring telecommunications in the classroom (Kurshan 1990). Although many are similar, what makes each unique is that it is tailored to a specific population's need and each often uses one of several incompatible 'networks' to link the classes. The interconnection (or compatibility) of networks is still an issue seeking resolution and, when solved, will go far to enlarging the telecommunications role in the curriculum.

Students from kindergarten through graduate school are beginning to use computers and telecommunications to break down cultural and geographic barriers, thus increasing their awareness of the interdependent world and their own roles in it. For example, the traditional cultural isolation of American students has been reduced through telecommunications projects. By exposing students in the United States directly to the viewpoints of students in other countries, and vice versa, the cultural filtration of information is minimised and the shared international experience replaces the typical parochial point of view. American classes have linked with students in the UK, Austria, Germany, Japan, Finland, Australia, Sweden and Iceland to discuss issues such as acid rain, German unification, international news, language usage, literature, history, and cultural themes and comparisons.

AN APPLICATION OF TELECOMMUNICATIONS

To meet the challenge of appropriately using telecommunications in education, the School of Education of the City College of the City University of New York developed a curriculum-based programme jointly with the Education Department at the Polytechnic of the South Bank and supported by the Institute of Education at the University of London and the Polytechnic of North London. As facilitators, co-ordinators, curriculum developers and teacher trainers, these higher-education institutions invited schools at all pre-college levels to participate in the Global Education Telecommunications Network project (GETN), designed and established to enable elementary and secondary students in many countries to exchange information and conduct joint research projects using personal computers.

New York City area public teachers and their classes in some forty elementary and secondary schools have, for the past two years, linked through electronic mail (e-mail) with their counterparts in Austria, Australia, England, Iceland, Finland, Germany, Japan and Sweden. Participating teachers have developed special classroom projects that enable their students to learn about other cultures, to communicate with students abroad, and to participate in inquiry-based learning projects. Children in classrooms around the world are collecting and sharing data, expressing their views, and discussing real and pressing issues. The goal of the project is to utilise telecommunications technology and international collaboration to improve learning and instruction for participating school children.

To participate in GETN, a school needs to have a computer, printer, modem, and an available telephone line (although not necessarily designated exclusively for this use). While most schools already have the first two, many still have to acquire modems and phone lines. Communications software is also needed to connect to the network. Each school is given a mailbox (identification number) on the system permitting the schools to access the network and begin communication. The communications network used in this project is Dialcom (BT Tymnet), a service that not only offers the capacity to send and receive messages, but also has a variety of databases available (e.g. AP News, Dow Jones, International News, etc.) that can help students and teachers search for information for a particular project. As teachers join the programme, they receive training in using the software and the network system. In addition, they are enrolled in graduate-level courses designed to help them develop curricula for the projects, review and evaluate the educational uses of telecommunications, and learn about telecommunications technology with its many current applications and future potential uses.

GETN fosters increased communications and dialogue among students via e-mail while it motivates interest in the latest telecommunications technology. More importantly, the curricula projects developed in GETN engage students in a full range of activities including reading, writing, reviewing, reporting, and publication as well as mathematics and scientific applications. These activities support the findings of researchers that indicate technology enhances traditional school learnings as well as problem solving and technology skills development (Levin, Rogers, Waugh and Smith 1989).

GETN also provides other significant enrichments to the learning process because it raises interesting, important, and 'real' questions that can be researched by participating classes, allowing students to do relevant and meaningful work; it initiates learning as meaning-making, constructive and active rather than passive; it results in meaningful and useful end products; it facilitates students' roles as the producers of knowledge; and it gives them a sense of ownership through the sharing and exhibition of their work.

There are currently ten model projects that were initially created by teachers involved in GETN. These projects have now been further developed and systematised at the City College of New York by participating teachers and college faculties in order that teachers anywhere in the world can participate in them. Special material packets for each project are being produced and will include: project description, welcome packet ideas, project objectives, suggested project activities, appropriate resource materials, and evaluation guidelines. These material packets are crucial for structuring and guiding teacher and student participation in each of the projects. A sample of model projects that were developed are:

- *A visitors guide to New York and London (or other city).* Students visit and do research about sites in New York and communicate with students doing a parallel project in London. Students describe their field trips and create a visitor's guide. This project not only teaches students about a city in another country, but it also teaches them more about their own city. The motivation of this timely international sharing of information serves to stimulate the learning process in a number of disciplines.
- *Immigration.* Students study issues related to immigration. They interview classmates, parents, and/or relatives to compare how immigration has affected different age groups, to learn about the reasons for immigration, and to determine the problems and experiences new immigrants have after arriving in New York (or any city). Additional research about immigration is obtained from a variety of sources including books, articles, and visits to a US Immigration Service facility. A comparison of immigration patterns and problems with students in other countries will enrich the study of this topic and strengthen its understanding.
- *International newsletter.* Links with classrooms in Austria, England, Finland, Germany, Iceland, Japan, Sweden, the United States and other countries result in a newsletter. Newsletters contain current events, sports, local and school news, cultural traditions, and fashion trends and are produced bi-weekly by a different country on a rotating

basis. These newsletters produced by students are shared with students in each participating city and become part of language arts, geography, current events, and global studies lessons. This activity enables students to actively engage in a meaningful sharing activity with students in other cultures.

- *Acid rain.* Students become involved in testing water samples from a variety of sources for acidity. They use the samples to determine what impact the acidity has on the environment and compare data, issues, and possible solutions with co-researchers in classrooms of other countries. Students have an opportunity to collaborate within their own classroom, as well as with students around the globe, discussing acid rain and how it affects the environment. This discussion can be approached from a political, social, economic, or other dimension, depending on the mutually agreed upon usage by the teachers at the various sites.

- *Creative writing.* Students create a multicultural literary journal to include poems, short stories, and essays written by students in classrooms in various countries. Some of the writing is started by the students in one country and then completed by students in another country. In addition, students are comparing the way fairy tales (or folk tales) are told in their country with that in other countries. This project encourages students to improve their own writing skills as well as to compare the use of the English language with students in other countries. Very often the students prepare a 'glossary of terms' to help students in other countries better understand the writing projects.

- *River project.* Students compare water samples of the Hudson River, the River Thames, the Danube River (or other major rivers) and explore causes of pollution and possible solutions. Students conduct additional research to learn about the historical uses of the rivers and the effect of pollution on their use as a recreational facility, travel route, and/or a food source. This project gives students an opportunity to visit their local rivers, learn about geography, history, science and data collection, and become more aware of international rivers. In addition, this gives students further opportunities to improve their writing skills as they report their findings to students in other countries.

- *Trends and lifestyles.* Students in European and American classes explore similarities and differences in social, cultural, and fashion trends today and twenty-five years ago. After interviewing their parents, reading journals/books on the 1960s, and viewing films and television shows, participants become more familiar with life in the previous generation. This project gives students an opportunity to compare their way of life with that of their parents when they were

teenagers. In addition, the international comparison adds an interesting and unique dimension in that it allows students not only to
compare lifestyles in two generations but also in a variety of countries
during those years.

- *Current events.* Students compare the way the news is reported in the
  UK, Europe, and American newspapers and other media. The e-
  mail exchanges focus on the attitudes and beliefs about current events
  held by the various nations. This project encourages students to read
  newspapers and become familiar with current events and journalism.
  They also learn the way to analyse critically the manner in which
  news is perceived and for what reasons it is perceived differently in
  various countries. Students often learn that what is important news
  in one country is given little coverage in another.

- *Teenage issues and concerns from the teenagers' perspective.* Students survey
  teenage social behaviours, mores, beliefs about parenting, parent-
  hood, relationships, and work. Through the use of questionnaires,
  interviews, videos, and journal articles, students in various countries
  collect information about these issues. They compare their data with
  those in other cultures and provide solutions for some of the problems
  of teenagers around the world.

- *Employment survey.* Students study employment opportunities for those
  graduating/leaving secondary schools here and abroad. They visit
  employment agencies, read the classified advertisements in the news-
  paper, and talk to employees to determine the skills/requirements
  needed for certain jobs. Participants also compare the kind of pre-
  employment preparation students are given in their schools for entry-
  level jobs in technology skills, clerical office skills, automotive repair,
  and the arts. Information about job interviews, pre-employment testing, and salaries is also shared, thus giving students a better understanding of the international employment market and opportunities.

The GETN project has given students an opportunity to share their
work with students in other countries. Knowing that their work is being
shared with 'real' audiences has motivated students to put forward more
effort as they complete the work. Teachers have reported that writing
skills have improved as a result of this project.

GETN also gives students and teachers considerable prestige since
they are involved in an innovative, international learning experience.
An observation of the schools that are involved in GETN shows that
there is a major impact on the school's climate. The international
projects are displayed on bulletin boards around the school; newsletters
have articles about the GETN project; and students and teachers have
made presentations at local educational meetings. The presence of

GETN seems to generate a positive learning environment throughout the schools.

The GETN project has also given teachers an opportunity to discuss educational issues/methods on-line. Since the initial project development was first discussed by the participating teachers, there has been an opportunity for teachers to gain a global understanding of schools and the educational process. The project has also encouraged teachers to develop a better understanding of the importance of using active, meaningful, inquiry-based instruction in the context of sharing ideas with an international audience. As a result, teachers have become more professionalised as authors, conference presenters, and curriculum developers. Such activities have a positive spin-off to classroom work.

Although telecommunications networks are emerging in various parts of the world, some of these projects are only electronic 'pen-pal' experiences. The GETN approach is different and has a number of advantages, chief of which is a clear educational philosophy that supports the development of inquiry-based projects which are participant driven. That is, the telecommunications is merely a means to an end, while the curricular work is the primary focus. Naturally, the use of this modern technology gives students a genuine opportunity to become familiar with systems which will likely be part of their everyday lives in years to come.

The success of GETN to date, can be seen by its innovative contributions to the development of a more stimulating educational experience. As instructional applications of telecommunications technology are expanded and more fully developed, more students, schools and countries will be added to the GETN network, thereby expanding educational opportunities. By linking curriculum development with technology, GETN enhances student problem-solving, intellectual growth and collaborative learning. It is not unreasonable to expect that programmes such as GETN, which use technological advances as they become available, may point the way for educational cooperation into the next century.

FINDINGS FROM EARLY EXPERIENCES

Several issues must be addressed if telecommunications programmes are to be successful. In our experience with the GETN programme, we found teacher training to be of primary importance. Projects should succeed if teachers are comfortable with both the technical and curriculum aspects of the programme. Teacher-training programmes should include courses which will prepare teachers to use the computer in the classroom, both as a word processor and as a telecommunications instrument, introduce them to electronic networks, develop their ability to search for information through electronic databases and develop skills in messaging and conferencing. Above all, teacher training should address a key notion that, to some measure, this international technological application determines its direction from its own experiences.

As part of their technical repertoire, teachers also need to understand the basic components of telecommunications. This would include understanding the use of a computer in general and as a word processor, the function of a modem, telephone, and communications software. On-line etiquette skills, often taken for granted, should also be emphasised since, with cultural differences, an insensitivity here can cause projects to fail.

In-service training courses were also found to have met another very important need. Teachers developed pedagogical skills, heretofore untapped, which linked telecommunications applications to general curriculum development. These pedagogical skills were most successful when focused on the development of projects which included cross-curricular instruction and internationally provocative topics.

A form of orientation must also be provided to principals and other supervisors to assure that they fully understand, and can be supportive of, these telecommunications projects on a school-wide basis. With their support, the creation of a time period within the school programme to accommodate a telecommunications strand as an integral part of the curriculum can be more easily realised. When an entire school community felt a sense of ownership of the GETN project, the project seemed to enjoy a far greater degree of success.

Educational e-mail projects also need careful coordination and management. In GETN, a university faculty member is designated to co-ordinate the programme, providing curriculum support for individual school projects and collaborating with the primary and secondary schools to establish international links for the participating classes. Teachers need a resource which will help to provide them with these links, help them in the technological aspects of the work, and offer some general support as they develop their projects.

As part of its co-ordination responsibilities, the university needs carefully to monitor the participating schools and their activities. In addition, dissemination of information about the project, such as evaluation reports, the development of training manuals, the creation of new links, and the preparation of user lists should also be part of the project coordination. International conferences provide further co-ordination and new linkages which are needed to keep injecting more 'life' into the programme.

Finally, if e-mail is to be effective, projects should be designed with specific goals, activities and outcomes, compatible with age/grade level and subject/topic areas. This can be achieved by having teachers 'talk' on-line before any project begins. In the GETN programme, the most successful projects had extensive student participation in the planning process. A project timeline with beginning and ending dates should also be prepared, specifically setting deadlines for data collection and transmission. Once the projects are completed, the results and evaluation of the experience, should be shared.

The teachers who participated in GETN projects agreed that there were several pedagogical reasons for implementing telecommunications into the existing curriculum. They concluded that telecommunications facilitated several educational objectives including: increased international understanding, the encouragement of respect for cultural differences, highly motivated learning through the timely sharing of information with a real audience, attaining technological skills whose uses extend beyond the classroom, learning in a content-integrated environment, a genuine opportunity to engage in inquiry-based learning, and the enrichment of the school curriculum.

ASSESSMENT OF A TELECOMMUNICATIONS PROJECT

Educational programmes are traditionally assessed by the actual knowledge and skills students acquire and/or by changes in their affective behaviours resulting from a particular set of learning activities. Although it would be possible to assess some telecommunications activities in terms of cognitive achievement, it is believed that the goals and characteristics of telecommunications programmes more properly point to assessment, focusing on both teacher and student attitudes and on the learning process. For example, has this international intervention motivated students sufficiently to increase their receptivity to other, more traditional learning modes? Has the use of this technology rejuvenated teachers to a point where their attitudes toward their instruction has motivated them to be more effective in the classroom? Has the range, concentration, and treatment of topics studied been increased to a point where learning becomes more meaningful? Has the mode of instruction had the spin-off effect of making both students and teachers able to deal with the technologically advancing society more easily and with less anxiety? Does this medium enable students to get a better understanding of other cultures and ideas so as to better understand their own? These and other related questions should form the basis of an evaluation. A traditional 'programme evaluation' may be inappropriate in a non-traditional programme.

The experience of GETN teachers has consistently been that involving students in meaningful learning activities via telecommunications strengthens instruction dramatically. Students are far more motivated to read materials that they get from 'colleagues' abroad and are excited about responding to them through writing. They know that their work and efforts will reach a receptive peer audience. Written work that is shared through computer networks is received in a form that can be easily read, revised, and reprinted. Instruction in academic subject areas is brought to life through student-to-student dialogues (Cohen and Riel 1989).

Telecommunications is now beginning to alter the approach to education; and as the technology advances, telecommunications will play a key role in bringing the latest information to students, whether from national or international peer audiences or established databases. Theodore Sizer (1985) views 'students as workers', who in the realistic, and meaningful forum, provided here by advanced telecommunications linkages, will achieve their educational goals more effectively than in years before these technological provisions existed. It can be expected that within the next few years, with increased technological support and with increased familiarity by educators, student learning will be enhanced and enriched through active involvement in real projects, resulting in personal satisfaction and improved achievement.

REFERENCES

Barbour, A. (1987), 'Restructuring of schools urged at conference examining school technology', *Electronic Learning*, January, pp. 9–11.

Binnard, W. '(1987), 'Computer learning month', *T.H.E. Journal*, October, pp. 88–92.

Bozeman, W. C. and House, J. E. (1988), 'Microcomputers in education: the second decade', *T.H.E. Journal*, February pp. 82–6.

Bracey, Gerald W. (1988), 'Computing at risk: students get bad grade on first report card', *Electronic Learning*, September, pp. 36–7.

Charp, S. (1987), 'Editorial', *T.H.E. Journal*, May, p. 10.

Clark, R. E. and Gavriel, S. (1976), 'Media in teaching', *Second Handbook on Research of Teaching*, Chicago, Rand McNally Publishing Company, pp. 464–74.

Cohen, M. and Riel, M. (1989), 'The effect of distant audiences on students' writing', *American Educational Research Journal*, Summer, pp. 143–59.

Colborn, C. (1989), 'Calling all schools!', *Teachers and Computers*, May-June, pp. 20–4.

Crowley, M. L. (1989), 'Organizing for electronic messaging in the schools', *The Computing Teacher*, April, pp. 23–6.

DeKock, A. and Paul, C. (1989), 'One's district's commitment to global education', *Educational Leadership*, September, pp. 46–9.

Electronic Learning, (1989), 'Teacher education: new ideas for professional development – a report of EL's second annual technology leadership conference', *Electronic Learning*, November, pp. 22–8.

Ferguson, S. and Strivens, J. (1988), 'Evaluation of the Red Hill/Marion Street E-Mail Project', University of Liverpool, Department of Education.

Gersh, S. O. (1990), 'Global education telecommunications network', paper presented in Luxemburg at the European Community conference 'Telematics: an opportunity for intercultural learning and communication.' March.

Hannafin, M. J., Dalron, D. W., and Hooper, S. R. (1987), 'Computers in education: barriers and solutions', *Educational Media and Technology Yearbook*, pp. 5–18.

Hutcher, P. (1990), 'SchoolLink: telecommunications transforms distance learning', *T.H.E. Journal*, May, pp. 72–4.

Kurshan, B. (1990), 'Educational telecommunications connections for the classroom – part 1', *The Computing Teacher*, April, pp. 31–5; part 2, pp. 51–2.

Levin, J. A., Rogers, A., Waugh, M., and Smith, K. (1989), 'Observations on electronic networks: appropriate activities for learning', *The Computing Teacher*, May, pp. 17–21.

Lewis, P. H. (1989), 'E-mail searches for a missing link', *New York Times*, 12 March, F6.

Madian, J. (1990), 'In the midst of restructuring, our only hope is a knowledgeable teacher', *Electronic Learning*, March, pp. 8–9.

Mageau, T. (1990), 'Telecommunications in the classroom: four teachers' stories', *Teaching and Computers*, May – June, pp. 18–24.

McCarthy, R. (1988a), 'Educational software: how it stacks up,' *Electronic Learning*, April, pp. 26–30.

——(1989), 'The advantages of using a network', *Electronic Learning*, September, pp. 32–8.

——(1988b), 'Making the future work – the road to curriculum integration', *Electronic Learning*, September, pp. 42–6.

Melvin, T. (1988), 'A computer project links students with soviet partners', *New York Times*, 4 December, pp. A1, 20.

Newman, D. (1990), 'Opportunities for research on the organizational impact of school computers', *Educational Research*, April, pp. 8–13.

Pearlman, R. (1989), 'Technology's role in restructuring schools', *Electronic Learning*, June, pp. 8–9, 12, 14–15, 56.

Reed, S. and Sautter, C. (1987), 'Visions of the 1990s: what experts predict for educational technology in the next decade', *Electronic Learning*, May – June, pp. 18–23.

Ross, S. M., Smith, L. J., Morrison, G., and Erickson, A. (1989), 'Helping at-risk children through distance tutoring: Memphis ACOT', *T.H.E. Journal*, February, pp. 68–71.

Schrum, L. (1988), 'Telecommunications: a window to the world', *Instructor*, October pp. 31–2.

Sculley, J. (1988), 'Tools for the future', *T.H.E. Journal*, Macintosh Special Issue, p. 10.

Shaloy, M. L. (1987), 'Sunburst's Marge Kosel: striving to set the software standard', *Electronic Learning*, January, pp. 24–5.

Sigliano, J. A., Joslyn, D., and Levin, J. (1989), 'The non-school learning environment: ECR', *T.H.E. Journal*, February, pp. 63–7.

Simon, M. (1988), 'Let's help teachers harness computer power', *Electronic Learning*, March, p.6.

Sizer, T. R. (1985), *Horace's Compromise: the dilemma of the American high school*, Boston, Massachusetts, Houghton Mifflin Co.

Takeshi, U., Rossman, P. and Rosen, S. (1989), 'Global education for the 21st century: the GU Consortium', *T.H.E. Journal*, March, pp. 75–7.

Tinker, R. F. (1989–90), 'Telecomputing for all', *Hands On!*, Winter, pp. 2, 15.

White, M. (1989), 'Educators must ask themselves some important questions', *Electronic Learning*, September, pp. 6, 8.

Wrigley, G. (1988), 'Telecommunications planning guide for educators', *The Computing Teacher*, November, pp. 24–9.

10

A coherent response to the challenge of technology from schools and higher education in the UK

GEOFFREY HARRISON

INTRODUCTION

Education is notorious for its inertia. The time scale of change is vast. The emergence of the National Curriculum in England and Wales, finally triggered by a radical administration in 1985, will only produce its first fully influenced graduates in the year 2006.

Even this particular programme is an exceptional case of extreme haste. For technology, the time span to bring about influence should be seen as extending back to the early 1960s when the British government perceived the need to do something to meet the needs of a twentieth-century technological society and took steps, through the Schools Council, to launch Project Technology and attempted to change things by persuasion. Over the following twenty-five years several other initiatives evolved within the education service, in response to the perceived need for individuals to be better prepared for exercising their technological capabilities to their full potential.

These initiatives, being largely independent of each other, have emerged as dislocated influences on inconsistent sections of the population. They have come from sources with very differing philosophies and objectives, each having their own power bases and financial backing. Their individual effects are diverse; their combined effect is inefficient. However, it is now possible to observe an emerging consensus which, if it can become instrumental in establishing coherence, could significantly enhance the overall impact on the quality of education.

This chapter identifies some of the principal contributory strands of educational changes which have been taking place and it relates them to the power bases of the organisations and programmes which have been developing them. The emerging conclusion is that the ultimate quality of the education of individuals will be dependent on an holistic approach to education and training which avoids the traps of centralised bureaucracy but provides a coherence of sense of purpose; avoids the false dichotomy between 'education' and 'training' but seeks to expand the abilities of individuals; and avoids a bigoted persistence in calling for 'traditional values' but sets unambiguous standards of achievement as targets to be aimed at by teachers.

DEVELOPMENTS AND INITIATIVES FROM THE RECENT PAST

To learn from the past it is necessary to set boundaries in time; while we must be conscious of the philosophies and exhortations from Plato to Bacon and to Arnold, our own times provide sufficient materials on which to work and build plans for the future. The historical boundaries for the purpose of this paper, therefore, run from the Crowther Report, *15 to 18*, of 1959[1] (which itself was set in the context of the UK 1944 Education Act with its expectation of tripartite schools providing 'each according to his needs') to 1990 with the emergence of the National Curriculum, Technical Vocational Educational Initiative (TVEI)[2] extension to all pupils, and enterprise emerging as a feature of higher education.

Over this period there have emerged philosophies, practices, political initiatives and industrial and commercial pressures, and a teaching force torn between wanting clarity of direction and welcoming freedom to do things in their own way. These have issued from diverse groups each with their own interests and perspectives. The result is that we now have a plethora of experiences and evidence on which to base more objective planning and guidance for the future. What has emerged can be seen from three aspects.

Firstly there are the philosophies and ideals; then there are the political and instrumental initiatives; and then there are the practical developments by individual educators, at all levels, with or without political and institutional support.

PHILOSOPHIES AND IDEALS

The alternative road

The Crowther Report, entitled *15 to 18*, was the consequence of a national committee of enquiry into the education of young people in the UK over the three years from the end of compulsory schooling. Chapter 35 of the Crowther Report is entitled 'The alternative road' and points out that: 'It (academic tradition) is not, however, the only road by which good minds can travel. If the country is to benefit fully from the intelligence of all its able boys and girls it will be necessary to rehabilitate the word 'practical' in educational circles – it is often used in a pejorative sense – and to define it more clearly.'

This chapter was written, largely, by Dr Frazer of Gateway School, Leicester, and was drawn from the experience of the pioneering technical high schools arising from the 1944 Education Act. These schools had developed a technological philosophy which they found gave a raison d'être for their whole curriculum. This technological philosophy was picked up by Project Technology, the curriculum development project launched by the Schools Council in 1966[3] and further developed by the School Technology Forum in the 1970s[4]. It also formed the basis of a second Schools Council project in the late 1970s.

The essence of that philosophy is that technology is a disciplined process which calls on the available and new resources of knowledge and understanding and which seeks to achieve human needs and wants. It views technology, therefore, as being the instrument of human advancement and not its result. It is, therefore, bound up with human values and value judgements. It is this three-part philosophy – human values and purpose; the active processes of achievement; and the resources of understanding and skill – which have provided an underlying philosophy and framework for much of the practical planning which has emerged during the 1970s and 1980s.

Education for capability

In the early 1980s the Royal Society of Arts launched its Manifesto for Education for Capability.[5] The RSA has issued awards for developments in schools which match up to this manifesto. It has also addressed the question of 'capability' in higher education, particularly for engineering.[6] These emerging philosophies of education for technological capability led to many questions about the purpose of education. Why was education not already aiming to foster capability? Or was it, by other names and by other means? Research indicated some fundamental changes in pupils' attitudes to technology were brought about through engagement in creative technological activities.

They also bred confusion in the minds of teachers, at all levels, who preferred to see their own function in more clear-cut terms of fostering understanding and skills on a narrower front. School science education[7] and engineering higher education[8] were particularly sensitive to any pressures for change. These, and similar, philosophies started to appear, implicitly at least, in many of the political and instrumental developments of the 1970s and 1980s.

This period has seen many initiatives, the driving purposes of which have not been so much philosophical as political and expedient.

Project Technology

Project Technology itself was a response by the government to the perceived need for a population able to cope with the 'white heat of the technological revolution' in which it found itself. The project was under pressure from many sides. For instance, industry saw the need for obedient highly skilled workers; the engineering profession recognised its low status and wanted the project to concentrate on producing more high-quality engineers; while educators wanted something with a more solid sociolgical and cultural base. Such persistent pressures overlooked the fact that teachers, on the whole, do not willingly see their role as producing 'industry fodder' to increase the profits of shareholders. The philosophy of 'enterprise' was not yet acceptable; neither had the concept of personal all round capability yet been accepted as a prime criterion for selection into industrial appointments.[9]

Government aid

In the 1970s, government departments in the UK stretched their financial regulations to provide support to the schools. While they were not allowed to provide direct educational support they did provide schools with information about, for example, the industrial technologies, energy efficiency and engineering activities in general. Treasury rules also, perhaps paradoxically, prevented the Department of Education and Science from influencing the content of the school curriculum. That responsibility had been passed to the Schools Council.

An internal move by HMI (Her Majesty's Inspectors) initiated a major national debate, not only about the purposes, and the social expectations, of education but also about the instruments and methods available to society and the government to have direct influence on the content of the curriculum, in schools and in higher education.[10] The opening gambit in this new role for government was Prime Minister James Callaghan's speech at Ruskin College, Oxford, in October 1976:

'The goals of our education, from nursery school through to adult education, are to equip children to the best of their ability for a lively, constructive place in society and also to fit them to do a job of work. Not one or the other, but both.' It was followed by the newly found freedom of HMI to publish discussion papers about the nature and content of the curriculum.[11] These were shortly followed by policy documents from the department itself.

Nevertheless, such documents could only inform and advise. It was still not permissible for the DES to provide tangible support for the school curriculum and to move it in any particular direction. It was only with the 1988 Education Reform Act that the department was given such influence. The National Curriculum, which follows from the Act, places technology firmly in the curriculum for *all* pupils from the age of 5 to 16.

This autonomy of the schools was matched by the independence of engineering departments within an autonomous higher education system. Individual courses had to meet the high academic standards set by their own institutions (in the case of universities) and by the Council for National Academic Awards (in the case of polytechnics and colleges). In practice, they also had to meet the criteria laid down by the professional institutions (the Institutions of Mechanical Engineering, Civil Engineering, etc.) through their Council of Engineering Institutions which was the route for registering and giving professional engineers chartered status. On the whole, engineering degree course teachers saw themselves as providing future engineers with the science they would need. They saw the development of engineering capabilities, as such, being the job of employers.

Several moves, from the 1960s onwards, produced recommendations for change, including the Willis Jackson report of 1966[12] which sought to distinguish between the scientific and the technological needs of future engineers and even recommended the broadening of undergraduate engineering courses. The particularly specialist nature of engineering degree courses was seen as being a significant reason for low recruitment and poor later industrial performance.

- The committee was: 'impressed by the project work illustrative of engineering and technology which is being introduced in many schools'.
- The committee saw the need to: 'foster the utilisation of 'non-academic' talents not at present selected by the educational system'.
- Engineering and technology should be presented, in schools, as:

'creative activities involving not only the application of science but also the resolution of complex economic and sociological problems'.

- In higher education, the Committee recommended that means should be formed to support: 'those who evince high abilities . . . in the knowledge of how to design, plan and synthesise, etc.'
- A decade later, the Department of Industry produced a report[13] which identified serious deficiencies in the approach to engineering which: 'tends to be treated simply as a branch of science (and an inferior one at that) and that its status would be enhanced if it was distinguished more sharply from science'.

The report condemned attitudes in universities which lacked interests in the vocational aspects of engineers. At the same time as this report was published. Sir Monty Finniston was invited by the Secretary of State for Education and Science to chair an inquiry into the engineering profession. The appointment, in 1977, of this committee of inquiry to look at the nature of the whole of the formation system for future engineers, was the first direct governmental intervention at this level.

The committee assembled evidence not only from higher education itself but also from industry, the school sector and the professional institutions. Amongst many other matters the final report, *Engineering Our Future*,[14] identified the nature of what it called the 'engineering dimension' which it considered essential for inclusion in all engineering courses. This 'dimension' covered the whole field of reality, from familiarity with engineering materials and design to the application of theory to practice and to the industrial and economic necessities of engineering. Although there was a change in administration, the government of the day largely accepted the recommendations of *Engineering Our Future* and created the Engineering Council not only to manage the Register of Chartered and Technical Engineers but also to provide a central controlling influence on the nature of courses designed to educate future engineers.

PRACTICAL DEVELOPMENTS

In addition to these more formal developments, there have been many initiatives by individual teachers and institutions which have been excellent in themselves but which have never been part of the established educational system. In the 1960s the Page Report *Engineering Among the Schools*,[15] and *A School Approach to Technology*, written by Don Porter, HMI, for the Schools Council[16] both listed details and rationales of such individual practical developments.

The establishment by Project Technology of the National Centre for School Technology (NCST) at Trent Polytechnic, (now Nottingham Polytechnic)[17] provided a central resource to continue the earlier thrust towards changing the curriculum. Later NCST became part of what is now the Trent International Centre for School technology at Nottingham Polytechnic. In higher education, individual engineering departments, such as that at the Polytechnic of the South Bank, have committed their courses to a basis of design projects. The developments at Heriot Watt University, Edinburgh during the 1970s laid the foundation for design-based structured learning in civil engineering. These, however, are exceptions rather than the rule and such courses tended to run up against externally imposed criteria for validation and acreditation.

CURRENT DEVELOPMENTS

Independent initiatives

Radical changes in recent years are now emerging at the point where the earlier philosophies and policies are becoming institutionalised. There is, at last, the possibility that these changes, in different phases of education, can be mutually supportive and continuous and thereby enhanced in their effect. It will be necessary, now, to ensure that the details of continuity, such as in flexible learning styles, educational aims and objectives, assessment for formative, selective, summative and recording and reporting purposes are, actually, consistent with each other and are easily perceived and understood. Both the Engineering Council and the Council for National Academic Awards have developed policies and criteria to be met by all courses intending to prepare students for professional or Chartered Engineer status.

Quotations for these might be seen in parallel.

Engineering Council, SARTOR[18]

'Any distinction between "theoretical" and "practical" courses is unreal in this context; each course should embody and integrate theoretical, practical and project work commensurate with the level of study being pursued. Also, the convenience and familiarity of traditional examining

CNAA policies[19]

'potential for success in an engineering career is not to be judged by academic ability alone and *entry to such courses must be based upon assessment of a wide student profile.*'

methods must not be allowed to inhibit course development or dictate teaching methods and syllabuses.'

'One essential element of engineering education is the "techne" quality or an appreciation of the engineering dimension. This implies the perception of a need, the knowledge to satisfy it, the capability of creating an artefact or engineering system with the necessary performance and the ability to sell it. This is a quality which needs to be developed and built on throughout an engineering degree course.'

... 'The selection of candidates for engineering courses should take account of all the qualities listed: 'human skills, academic qualities, mathematical skills, knowledge skills and also *an engineering dimension or "techne" quality*'. '... The academic qualities are commonly used for selection because they can be measured by examinations'.

These formalised requirements for Higher Education engineering courses emerged at about the same time as the government of the day was considering how it might make the school curriculum become more relevant to the needs of economic industry without losing the essence of general education. At the time the UK government was still hampered by the financial inability of the Department of Education to intervene directly in the curriculum. Other countries, such as Australia, had encountered the same sort of constitutional obstacles to central influence on education and were using direct funding tactics similar to those now being developed in the UK.[20]

In the UK the difficulty was overcome by channelling central government funds through a non-governmental body, the Manpower Services Commission. The system for this became known as the Technical and Vocational Education Initiative which funded, first, a series of pilot projects (for limited numbers of students) from which 'extension' projects are now developing for *all* students in all schools and colleges between the ages of 14 and 18.

This funding was to support any well-managed project which could be seen to achieve the aims and meet the criteria which had been laid down. With few exceptions, these aims and criteria were drawn up in very general terms. The purpose was to seek out imaginative ideas and support them rather than to provide central direction of a common programme. It was not intended that pupils should follow a wholly vocational curriculum. Rather, starting at age 14 with approximately 30 per cent of the curriculum being vocational, and ending up with 70 per cent at age 18 was what was expected. This, however, never became a substantive requirement. The following aims for TVEI were laid down in 1983 and remain the basis of the current funding policies:

> to give young people aged 14–18 access to a wider and richer curriculum so that:
>
> i)   more of them are attracted to seek the qualifications/skills which will be of direct value to them at work and more of them achieve these qualifications and skills;
>
> ii) they are better equipped to enter the world of employment which will await them;
>
> iii) they acquire a more direct appreciation of the practical application of the qualifications for which they are working;
>
> iv) *they become accustomed to using their skills and knowledge to solve the real-world problems they will meet at work, and in adult life;*
>
> v)   more emphasis is placed on developing initiative, motivation and enterprise as well as problem-solving skills and other aspects of personal development;
>
> vi) the construction of the bridge from education to work is begun earlier by giving young people the opportunity to have direct contact and planned work experience with local employers in the relevant specialisms;
>
> vii) there is close collaboration between local education authorities and industry/commerce/public services etc., so that the curriculum has industry's confidence.

It is aim number (iv) which most closely matches the philosophies for technology and capability mentioned earlier, while the principal changes brought about in the curriculum involved students in 'work experience' and an increase in average time spent in subjects such as technology and business studies.

An increase in the amount of time spent on these subjects did not necessarily mean a move towards a common philosophy of technology and capability. Evaluation reports on TVEI pilot projects are critical of the lack of grasp of the fundamental shift in aims which had been expected. Indeed, the very diversity of approach is seen as symptomatic of a subject under development and still lacking a tradition. The evaluation reports point out that there are some impressive manifestations of technology in the curriculum which are likely to become more widely established with the advent of the National Curriculum. In the meantime, much clearer thinking is needed about the teaching and learning of both the 'capability' and the 'awareness' aspects of technology.[21, 22, 23]

In preparation for the extension phase of TVEI, the training agency

issued a guidance paper on what might be expected in terms of technology in the participating schools and local authorities. This paper,
Technology for TVEI,[24] suggested a model for technology which was
identical with that developed by Project Technology and the School
Technology Forum twenty years previously and used consistently since
then.[25]

The extension phase of TVEI is more or less coincident with the
emergence of the National Curriculum, mentioned earlier. The subject
of technology is now a legal requirement in the education of all pupils
in UK-maintained schools. Key features of this new subject include the
following:

1 It comprises two 'capabilities': that for 'information technology' and
   that for 'design and technology'. The attainment targets for the latter
   match very well with the model for technological capability used by
   Project Technology and by TVEI.
2 It must involve pupils in technological activities in the business,
   economic and industrial communities as well as in those of the school
   and home. It therefore provides the framework on which to hang the
   cross-curricular requirement for education in business and economic
   awareness.
3 Its programmes of study have flexible contents but, such as there are,
   must be taken to the high level of understanding and application
   called for in the assessment targets.
4 Assessment is essentially based on the process activities of capability,
   viz. Identifying needs and opportunities; generating a design; planning and making; evaluating.

Even before the influence of the National Curriculum, there are many
instances of programmes, based in individual schools, or in consortia
of schools, where the philosophies of technology and capability have
been successfully pursued to the point of assessment by examinations
and project presentation. However, it is only recently that the success
or otherwise of TVEI has been able to be gauged by those who now
employ ex-TVEI students. They report a very strong approval of the
abilities and competencies of such students.[26]

Despite such obvious successes, several obstacles to a widespread
extension of achievement of the aims of TVEI have not yet been overcome. First of these is the difficulty of assessing capability in objective
terms. Second is the difficulty of placing evidence of assessment (such
as it is) in the context of more conventionally accepted examinations
(General Certificate of Secondary Education; Advanced Levels; etc.)
which carry the weight needed for acceptance into further and higher

education. This is particularly significant in the field of engineering. The lack of a good match, represented by assessment objectives, between the learning outcomes up to the age of 18 and the content and approach of engineering degree courses is most noticeable and was referred to earlier.

It is this interface between secondary and higher education, where the lack of a good match in terms both of coherence of learning objectives in the field of technological capability and of the motivation and career influence, where there is a potential for making a most significant advance in coherent education. The Manpower Services Commission, on behalf of the government, and using the same technique as for TVEI of making money available and inviting proposals for its expenditure, invited all institutions of higher education to achieve prescribed objectives using methods suggested by the institutions themselves. In this case it was called Enterprise in Higher Education (EHE) and money was offered to individual institutions on condition that corresponding funds (or their equivalent) were obtained from industry and commerce.

The objectives of EHE were as follows and many of the same antagonisms were experienced as in the case of the schools at the start of TVEI (these antagonisms, not surprisingly, faded away over the years as more money became available!).

The objectives of Enterprise in Higher Education[27] were as follows:

a) every person seeking a higher education qualification should be able to develop competencies and aptitudes relevant to enterprise;

b) these competencies and aptitudes should be acquired at least in part through project based work, designed to be undertaken in a real economic setting, and they should be jointly assessed by employers and the higher education institutions.

Many staff in institutions of higher education were reluctant to identify themselves with what had become known as the enterprise culture. However, in most cases 'enterprise' was acceptable when it was seen more as a matter of personal quality and initiative than representing the ability to make money. In some institutions it was the departments of fine and applied art that, most readily, responded to the opportunity.

The Department of Employment observed that the EHE initiative raised fundamental questions about learning and teaching and the nature of the curriculum, about competencies, assessment and accreditation and about the culture and ethos of higher education.[28] Some of the same difficulties over assessment have occurred in higher education as in the schools. (Although here there is the additional problem of the *entry* assessment, i.e. that which is used for selection of students onto the course.) Further difficulties occur in attempting to fit assessment of students' qualities of enterprise into the assessment methods approved by the validating body and the approving professional institution. Course tutors have been obliged to establish an active relationship between 'enterprise' and their traditional aims and objectives. Observing this relationship emerge in Nottingham Polytechnic has demonstrated the need for tutors to develop their own concept of 'enterprise' in relation to their aims, course content, and course structure. The evaluation of EHE is addressing this depth of penetration of enterprise into the ethos, practice and institutional structure of courses.

Coincidentally, some of the EHE initiatives are reflected in further recent developments in engineering courses following on the earlier policies of the Engineering Council and CNAA. There were perceived needs for more broadly based engineering degree courses and for providing access to engineering for a wider range of potential students. The Engineering Council produced a blueprint for such courses in its publication, *An Integrated Engineering Degree Programme*[29] This led to a number of pilot schemes being launched in polytechnics and universities supported by funding from the Department of Trade and Industry.

These courses are broader and less specialised than the normal engineering degree courses. They widen access without lowering standards. The only required Advanced-Level examination success is in mathematics. The recruitment to the integrated engineering degree course at Nottingham Polytechnic suggests that these courses are tapping a new field of potential engineering talent. The structure of the syllabus is integrated. Instead of having a large number of discrete disciplines, the syllabus is built on a small number of groups of disciplines using similar concepts, viz. information engineering; physical and chemical structures; processes and properties; mechanics, materials and structures; manufacturing; and enterprise, organisation and people. These are all brought together in the major section of the course called 'integrating studies'. All the integrating principles of the SARTOR document are embodied in this part of the course.

It is inevitable that tutors have had to think their teaching approaches afresh. Students are expected to: 'combine existing knowledge and skills in new ways and to go beyond the information given to tackle new problems sensibly and successfully. This concept in turn requires students to engage in a substantial amount of independent learning'. The emphasis is always on understanding a limited ranged of fundamental concepts to the level at which they may be applied to practical problems, rather than approaching a wider range of concepts at a more superficial level.

Coherent progression

From the foregoing, it is now possible to see common patterns emerging. These patterns are reflections of the purpose, process and resources aspect of capability which are common to TVEI, EHE, integrated engineering, etc. and are reflected in the emerging Core Skills concept of education for all, in the 16–19 age range. The planning for development of this phase of education and training is currently being influenced by the National Curriculum Council,[30] the Confederation of British Industry[31] and TVEI.[32] There is also an expectation that Advanced-level GCE examinations should be broadened and adapted to provide for a much larger sector of the population than hitherto, without losing any of the rigour and status of A Levels as they stand.

National Curriculum Council core skills	*CBI common learning outcomes*	*TVEI common learning outcomes*
communication	values and integrity;	All students should be able to:
problem-solving	effective communication;	communicate effectively (where possible in more than one language);
personal skills	applications of numeracy;	compile and use numerical information;
numeracy	applications of technology;	use science and technology appropriately;
information technology	understanding of work and the world;	understand the world of work;
modern language competence	personal and interpersonal skills;	develop effective personal and interpersonal skills;
	problem solving;	work independently and in teams;
	positive attitudes to change.	solve problems;
		cope positively with change.

CONCLUSION

It is now crucial that the coincidence of all these movements – in the schools up to the age of 16; in higher education (particularly in engineering); and the imminence of new approaches to education and training between 16 and 18 – should be seized upon. An effective 'matching section' needs to exist between the period of potential motivation towards capability, enterprise and technology (i.e. up to the age of 16), which capitalises on such motivation, and contributes towards it by recognising it and rewarding it with formal assessments and credit. And of most importance the student should be helped to feel that there is a continuity of learning; that concepts should be broad but taken to the level of practical application rather than deep esoteric study; that human values are of paramount importance and that this is reflected by their place in the curriculum and examinations.

But all this will require all parts of the system – tutors, students, employers, examiners and administrators – to come to a common understanding and purpose. Without it, each phase of education will be a law unto itself and unwilling to accept schemes, methods and philosophies 'not invented here'.

This calls for a general recognition that we have a new and common paradigm of learning to which all parties are prepared to subscribe. The Grubb Institute's report on TVEI extension[33] makes this point and insists that those concerned with administration of developments such as TVEI must work with the aims and the paradigm to the full. When these are lost to sight, importance is attached to the rhetoric of qualifications and institutional arrangements rather than the need to fulfil the agreed aims and objectives.

NOTES

1   *15 to 18*, (1959), (The 'Crowther Report'), Report of the Central Advisory Council for Education in England, Ministry of Education, HMSO.
2   TVEI was initiated by the Manpower Services Commission. As a result of governmental changes TVEI now comes directly under the auspices of the Department of Employment.
3   *Technology and the Schools: Working Paper No. 18* (1968), Schools Council, HMSO.
4   *School Technology Forum: Working Paper No. 1* (1973), Nottingham, Trent Polytechnic.
5   *Education for Capability: Recognition Schemes*, (1980), London, Royal Society of Arts.
6   *Engineering Futures: New Audiences and Arrangements for Engineering Higher Education* (1990), London, Engineering Council, in association with RSA and the Training Agency.

7   *Interpreters of Science: a History of the Association for Science Education* (1984), David Layton, John Murray.

8   *Engineering Among the Schools*, G. T. Page (1965), London, Institution of Mechanical Engineers.

9   *Craft, Design and Technology Links with Industry* (1980), Schools Council.

10 *Times Educational Supplement*, 15 October 1976.

11 *Curriculum 11–16: Working Papers by HM Inspectorate* (1977), Department of Education and Science.

12 *Report on the 1965 Triennial Manpower Survey of Engineers, Technologists Scientists and Technical Supporting Staff* (1966), HMSO.

13 *Industry, Education and Management: a Discussion Paper* (1977), Department of Industry.

14 *Engineering Our Future* (1980), Report of the Committee of Enquiry into the Engineering Profession. HMSO.

15 *Engineering Among the Schools*, G. T. Page (1965), London, Institution of Mechanical Engineers.

16 *A School Approach to Technology* (1967), Schools Council Curriculum Bulletin No. 2. Don Porter, HMI, HMSO.

17 On becoming independent of local authority control in April 1989, Trent Polytechnic became Nottingham Polytechnic.

18 *Standards and Routes to Registration* (1984), London, Engineering Council.

19 *Engineering First Degree Courses: a Policy Statement* (1984), London, Council for National Academic Awards.

20 *Participation and Equity in Australian Schools: the Goals of Full Secondary Education* (1984), Commonwealth Schools Commission, Canberra.

21 *The TVEI Curriculum 14–16: an Interim Report Based on Case Studies in Twelve Schools* in Barnes, Douglas and Johnson, George (1987), Sheffield, TVEI.

22 *Technology Projects in the Fifth Year*, Technology in TVEI. Medway, Peter and Yeomans, David Sheffield, TVEI.

23 *14–18: the Range of Practice* (1989), Technology in TVEI. Sheffield, TVEI.

24 *Technology for TVEI* (1987), London, Manpower Services Commission.

25 *Technology and the Schools: Working Paper No. 18* (1968), Schools Council, HMSO.

26 *Leaving TVEI and Starting Work: Employment Processes and Employer Reaction* (1989), London, Training Agency.

27 *Enterprise in Higher Education: Guidance for Applicants* (1988), London, Department of Employment.

28 *Key Features of the Enterprise in Higher Education Proposals* (1989), London, Department of Employment.

29 *An Integrated Engineering Degree Programme* (1988), London, Engineering Council.

30 *Core Skills 16–19* (1990), York, National Curriculum Council.

31 *Towards a Skills Revolution – a Youth Charter* (1989), London, Confederation of British Industry.

32 *Guidance for Preparing TVEI Extension Proposals for a 1991 Start* (1990), London, TVEI.

33 *Technical and Vocational Education Extension. Towards a Paradigm for Total Learning* (1989), The Grubb Institute.

11

Educating Rita – the real challenge: some reflections on a female and human approach to teaching technology

ANNE-MARIE ISRAELSSON

INTRODUCTION

It has long been the implied idea of educators all over the world that the female half of the world, given proper traditional training, would fit into the ready-made dress of the male engineer. Many projects have been invented and implemented at almost all levels of school and at university level with the expectation that female students would eagerly join technology classes and engineering schools, once their eyes had been opened to the wonders and possibilities of technology. Thus, the reluctance on the part of women, even those with proper basic education, to enter the field of technology, has remained a mystery. And as the strategy has not had the expected results, only more of the same kind has been applied, more persuasion, more 'special offers'.

But science and technology educators may have fallen into the same trap as did the college arts professor in the screen and stage success *Educating Rita* some years ago. Even arts people are stupid at times – so this professor thought all he had to do was educate Rita, bringing her to a proper level of knowledge and thus making her a happier human being, able to fit into the academic world. Educating Rita was even to him a real challenge – the task of a modern Pygmalion. But to Rita his world had nothing to do with real life, and the insight he gained from his educational endeavours with Rita was that this own conception of the world had to change.

Is there any hope that educators of technology have learnt from educating the many Ritas of this century to teach technology with a different – female and human – approach in the next century? How will the educational system and its representatives respond to the double challenge of the future: the demands of the rapidly changing technology and the needs of those to be educated – youth and adults, pre-school children and college students, men and women?

PROGRAMMES, FACTS AND FIGURES

Recruitment activities at the Luleå University of Technology, as everywhere in the world, were for a long time focusing on how to increase the proportion of female students within engineering. From 1976 onwards the Luleå University paid special attention to this particular problem by implementing information and recruitment programmes directed specially towards young girls, which was new and rather brave at that time. These programmes mostly intended to make those girls who had already chosen science in upper-secondary school aware of the opportunities in engineering, thus actually 'marketing' engineering as a future field of study and work. The activities proved, after some years of persistent work, to be rather successful. The Luleå University has from 1982 and ever since had the highest rate of female students among the institutes of technology in Sweden, ranging from 27 per cent in 1983 to almost 30 in 1987, whereas the national average never exceeded 20 per cent and is now about 18 per cent.[1]

During the course of this work I came to realise, however, that there was something fundamentally wrong in our way of attacking the whole problem of women and science and technology. There was too much of persuasion, of marketing technology in a way young women were supposed to 'fall for', just as if they would be stupid enough to do anything we wanted them to if we were clever in our marketing. We never really, during the first years of our activities, tried to find out why young girls were so reluctant to follow science and technology – we just wanted them to change. They had to change. We persuaded them to be more like the boys, to content themselves and even be happy with the way science and technology were taught in school, and at the university, and to accept and deal with the male dominance in the world of technology.

But considering the fact that women really are half of the population, the number of female students in engineering at Luleå and elsewhere would have been even larger, had things been as simple as we usually saw them: 'Every young person may choose his or her career freely and without restrictions.' Realising that this is not really the case, we began to be more careful about persuading girls to be pioneers in engineering. The core of the problem was obviously something else, and this 'something' required attention and a course of action.

For the last couple of years, numbers of female participation in engineering have actually been going down again, in western Europe as well as in the United States. This fact makes it all the more obvious that it is now time to focus instead on the reasons for women's rejection of science and technology.

SCHOOL REINFORCES TRADITIONAL ATTITUDES

There is no doubt that teaching practices at school are a crucial and strong factor in forming the attitudes of girls towards science and technology.

Initially, at the lower levels of school, the attitude of the girls towards science and technology is a positive one, just the same at that of the boys. This has been found in studies carried out at Linköping University.[2] We also found this to be true in our work during the developing phase of the science and technology centre Teknikens Hus, while we were experimenting with different methods to find out how to teach technology to young children in our hands-on exhibits and workshops. We did not see any difference in interest or enthusiasm between boys and girls at these lower age levels. But we noticed that the difficulties in attracting the interest of girls in secondary school increased the older the girls were. This in turn coincided with my experience at the university, where we tried to persuade girls from secondary school to opt for science in upper-secondary school, so that later they would be able to go on to engineering studies.

Boys generally, so we also found, are fascinated by technical devices and machines as such, not caring too much about the context as long as there is action. They can take an interest in a scientific principle expressed in an isolated course of events or be absorbed by minute wonders of technology – things which often leave girls cold. In most science teaching the principles, rules and basic concepts are taken apart – and the necessity of putting all these pieces together again and relating them to reality is more or less ignored in teaching practices. It is no surprise that boys are privileged and thus achieve well. The girls, on the other hand, are frustrated by the lack of context. Many science teachers have failed to realise that science teaching at school starts where the old scientists of yesterday finished, after they had been through their laboratory work and had been able from that to deduct, generalise and establish rules and principles. To them, the context was of course evident – it is not for girls in the twentieth century!

The nature of science itself has for long been analytical. Teaching and learning science and technology is also generally analytical and thus does not fit into the female way of conceiving reality as a whole. The deficiency of science teaching is thus related to science as such, as it has been practised through the centuries.

Girls will naturally get deterred and frightened when they realise that neither the teachers of science and technology nor the textbooks are adjusting teaching methods and teaching contents to the situation of girls and to their experience. This is true of both male and female teachers at higher levels of school, as they are all educated within the male world of science and technology. It is also true of most of the textbooks for different levels. This has been very clearly demonstrated in the works of several researchers in the project 'Girls and Physics' at the Centre for School Science, University of Oslo, Norway.[3]

NEW TEACHING METHODS PRACTISED AT TEKNIKENS HUS

However, my experience in developing exhibits and teaching practices in Teknikens Hus has convinced me that the female holistic approach to reality can be taken into account and used for teaching technology, by taking reality as a starting point for the learning process.

In Teknikens Hus we have taken reality into our exhibits by introducing industrial and technical environments which we suppose to be generally but superficially known to the children. Thus mining industry, steel industry and hydroelectric power production are each an exhibit area of their own in Teknikens Hus, all these technical and/or industrial areas being part of the regional environment. Other exhibit areas, e.g. water and how it is used as a source of power, a means of transportation etc., are linked to the industrial areas to form a true picture of the scientific and technical reality. Experiments and hands-on activities are performed in the context of where they belong, thus also explaining how things really work. Scales, of course, sometimes must differ from reality – and it is even easier to understand the whole process of steel making if it is not demonstrated in life size. Some teachers of technology in upper-secondary school claim that they now use Teknikens Hus for teaching about the whole process of steel-making on a small scale, before going for study visits to the steel works. The model scale steel works exhibit at Teknikens Hus then works well at a level of teaching for which it was not originally intended.

The teachers at Teknikens Hus also work with groups of children and teachers in workshops called 'The Kitchen', 'The Bathroom' and 'The Garage', where home technology is explored. These workshops are equipped and arranged in accordance with their designation, and the familiar setting makes it easier, especially to girls, to see the connection between technology and everyday life.

Girls as well as boys in this way relate to some of their own knowledge, e.g. about the industries of the region, often acquired through a parent or relative occupied in these industrial fields, or about the technology of everyday life. It has been very convincingly shown in the works of Professor Henning Johansson of Luleå University that connecting the teaching at school to the actual local and cultural environment of the children makes them learn quicker and with better results.[4] The feedback we get from teachers and parents – and from children writing to us after their visits – is very encouraging as to the effectiveness of our teaching methods. Often we find that an interest in science and technology, even with adults, has been born or revived.

TEACHER TRAINING A CRUCIAL FACTOR

A very important part of technology teaching is teacher training. I would like to draw special attention to the training of teachers for lower grades of school and for pre-school. Those teachers, mostly female, have a decisive impact on the attitude of both boys and girls to science and technology, especially as role models for girls at early ages. Teachers in pre-school and at lower levels of school receive little training in science and practically none in technology at college today, and this was certainly even more true in earlier years in Sweden. Many of these teachers have chosen their profession on the basis of a non-science/technology education in secondary school, and very often even as a means of avoiding technology. Science and technology have been considered difficult, boring and complicated by most of these teachers – obviously due in part to lack of good teaching in the earlier stages of their own education. They often opted out of science/technology at school and so are very frustrated when they have to teach those subjects.

In Teknikens Hus, we have been working with teacher in-service training for both pre-school and lower-secondary-school teachers. A study of the methods and an evaluation of the results of these training courses[5] has served as a background for further consideration and planning.

The evaluation shows that it has been possible to overcome the barrier of fear that most of these female teachers put up when even thinking of teaching science and technology. In our training courses we have given them a chance of acquiring practical experience in a familiar setting, e.g. the kitchen, and of working with different technical devices there. At the beginning, there was much fear and scepticism to overcome. After some time, though, and certainly after they had practised using their new knowledge and skills the development in this new area was very obvious. An important factor was the de-dramatisation of technology that was achieved by pointing at the existing technology in the everyday world – the kitchen, the bathroom etc. This helped the teachers see not only the close-at-hand technology but also the importance and use of knowing more about the technical devices we all use daily. From there, it was possible to widen the scope to see the inter-relationship between society and technology in issues like energy, transportation, environmental problems etc.

TEACHING AND TEACHERS FOR THE FUTURE

Not only the knowledge acquired, the achievement in science/technology by girls, and their interest in these subjects at school, is affected by teaching practices, but even more so the attitude of girls to science and technology generally and its role in our society. This attitude also depends on a number of other factors. Riis suggests in her study[2] that science and technology are seen as part of a patriarchal system and male-dominated network of power of our society and that this view might play an important role in the forming of girls' attitudes. Women and girls are not unaffected by what they see around them. Many of them today blame male society and male technology for the pollution and the devastation of our environment, for war and destruction of human values. Many girls, when asked, reject the mere thought of having anything to do with science and technology, which they see as inhuman and destructive.

My conclusion is simple: teaching at all levels of school must be changed. It is imperative that the situation of girls should be taken into account when planning the science and technology curriculum for the future. Questions relating to the conception of reality held by girls must be treated within the curriculum. Focusing on society as a whole and the implications of technology for our future is of great value to the whole of science and technology teaching – not just to the girls. It might be that boys would generally need more of the holistic approach to science and technology to be able to live and work in a changing world.

A holistic approach to teaching technology will also be vital to all those important issues on which decisions will have to be made by the citizens now and in the future. Many of these issues actually have technical components. How can we expect wise decisions from our future politicians or other decision makers, if we have failed to provide an education involving not only technology as such but also its use and its implications socially, environmentally and economically? This urge for a concerned science and technology is becoming more evident as time goes by.[6]

It is also necessary to change profoundly the science and technology teacher training for all school levels. This has led me to the controversial conclusion that children need teachers in science and technology with more of a *generalist* competence and *not* in the first place with more academic or specialist training. Those science and technology teachers trained in and marked by the traditional school of science have often had a detrimental effect on girl's interests and activities in these fields.

THE REAL CHALLENGE

Teachers nowadays are prepared for guiding the children into a very complicated world. Subject like war and peace, democracy, local and global environmental issues, cultural differences, minority problems etc. are and should be treated at school. But technology is almost excluded from the teacher's world – and yet technology is present everywhere.

Can we take responsibility of *not* trying to make our children feel secure in their everyday world? And how could they do so if, to many of them, the technical devices that surround them and the way these devices function, remain unfamiliar and even strange? How will the attitudes towards the roles of men and women in society ever change if children continue to grow up in a world – at home and in school – where females are ignorant and even hostile towards technology whereas technology is seen as powerful and important among male decision makers?

I would argue that a different approach to teaching science and technology is required for girls and that would also mean getting closer to fulfilling the needs of humanity. My final question will be: can we afford *not* to change our approach to teaching science and technology in a more female and thus human direction? These issues must be seriously discussed among scientists, technologists and educators concerned with the challenges of the future.

NOTES

1   Carlsson, Karin (1990), *The Percentage of Women on Study Programmes in Technology at Luleå and in the Rest of Sweden 1980–89*, Högskolan i Luleå, Luleå Sweden 1990.

2   Riis, Ulla (1989), 'Girls in science and technology', paper given at the 'Natur och Kultur' Symposium Science Education for the twenty-first Century at the Royal Swedish Academy of Sciences, Stockholm.

3   Sjöberg, Sven and Lie, Svein (1981), 'Girls and physics', contribution to GASAT–1, Eindhoven, The Netherlands, vol. 2; Lie, Svein and Bryhni, Eva (1983), 'Girls and physics: attitudes, experiences and under-achievement', contribution to GASAT–2, Oslo, Norway; Bryhni, Eva, and Lie, Svein (1985), 'Girls and the image of physics – an evil circle?', contribution to GASAT–3, London.

4   Johansson, Henning (1985), 'Culturally grounded elementary education', Umeå University, Umeå, Sweden.

5   Israelsson, Ann Marie and Nordell, Lennart (1990), 'Learning by doing – an old method still going strong', Contribution to GASAT, Jönköping, Sweden.

6   Lewis, John L. (1989), 'Science in society: impact on science education', paper Given at the 'Natur och Kultur' Symposium, Science Education for the 21st century, Royal Swedish Academy of Sciences, Stockholm.

12

The new technologists in higher education: where will they come from?

E. STINA LYON

It has become an annual feature of press reports on recruitment to higher education to express concern over the difficulties faced by institutions trying to bring students into technologically related subjects, especially engineering and associated disciplines. The need in the economy for technologists in a range of specialisms is growing, as is the more general need for graduate labour skilled in numeracy and computing and with a positive orientation towards key aspects of technological development. This need is reflected in the growth of salaries such graduates can command. Yet, an apparent paradox remains with prospective students continuing to apply in large numbers to non-technological subject areas, a situation not improved by what has come to be called 'the demographic time-bomb, of declining cohorts of school leavers entering higher education. Both higher education and the labour market will in these areas increasingly have to look for recruits amongst women graduates, mature graduates, and graduates from sectors in society not previously represented in higher education. There are many reasons why this task will not be an easy one despite the overall expansion of student numbers in higher education. It is the aim here to show that some of the problems to be faced go well beyond those of improved marketing of courses and the raising of salaries. These 'new' categories of students are, as I aim to show, not on the whole characterised by having the relevant educational background for the study of technology at the level of higher education, nor by career commitments which would make work in technologically demanding fields appear immediately attractive. To make matters worse, once in higher education students are not always helped, either to develop more general technologically relevant skills, (if they are on non-technologically oriented courses), or in their search for wider personal, educational development, if they choose a course in science or technology.

The relationship between an expanding higher-education system and changing labour market needs raises some general issues. The response of higher education to the recent challenge from employers to become responsive to their needs, have on the whole been to foster an approach of growing vocationalism. But, it will be argued, with graduates from all subjects and courses getting jobs with greater ease and income than students without degrees, albeit some quicker than others the issue of vocational orientation may be of less relevance to the immediate needs of the labour market for technologically informed labour, than the recruitment of students to relevant courses in the first place. The nature of access and recruitment to subjects and courses will then be discussed, with emphasis placed on the major differences in background qualifications which characterise students on different courses and in different institutions. This is one of the results of the tensions that exist between the social demand for places and the number of places offered within each possible 'profile' of entry qualifications. I will then turn to the nature of this demand, with special reference to the type of goals different kinds of students seek to have fulfilled through their higher-education experience, not all of which are labour market related. The final section will deal with the higher-education curriculum itself and the extent to which it can be seen to offer its students an opportunity to compensate for some of their earlier curriculum specialisations and shortages. I will conclude by raising the need for a closer look at the notion of a 'core' curriculum in higher education, an accepted concept in US undergraduate programmes. If, as has been noted, the structure and funding of the British system of higher education is going to share many of the features of the US system, then a closer look at the nature of its undergraduate as well as post-graduate system of education may be warranted (Williams 1989).

Evidence will be presented in support of the above from a few recent official research reports on student demand, subject choice and the relationship between higher education and the graduate labour market. I will also present evidence from a series of graduate surveys of the orientations, attitudes and experiences of graduates entering the labour market funded by the Council for National Academic Awards (CNAA) under the auspices of its Higher Education and the Labour Market Project (HELM). The Graduate Panel Survey was for a period located at the South Bank Polytechnic. It surveyed the transition into the labour market of samples of men and women from the 1982 and 1985 cohorts of CNAA graduates from a selection of courses in the polytechnic. The 1985 sample also included comparative groups of university and Business and Technician Education Council (BTEC) students. (For a more detailed discussion of the surveys and the findings, see Brennan and McGeevor 1988; Lyon, McGeevor and Murray 1988.) A final report of this project is forthcoming. It is not the aim here to discuss in detail the overall methodology and findings of the project, only to make selective use of some of the information it provides about students and their orientation to subject choice in higher education.

THE EXPANSION OF HIGHER EDUCATION AND THE LABOUR MARKET

The expansion of higher education in Britain continues. The participation rate has moved steadily upwards since the 1970s, and may soon approach 20 per cent. This expansion has been accompanied by the development of a greater diversity of courses and curricula, increasingly offered by institutions outside the traditional university sector. The demand for graduate labour in the economy is strong, as is the social demand for access to higher education of prospective students from a wider social, educational and age background than before. The drop in size of school-leaver cohorts, and the growing demand for highly qualified labour, has led the government to support an expansion of student numbers, though with the cost of such an expansion seen to be coming largely from the students themselves. It is still perhaps an exaggeration to talk of 'mass' higher education in Britain, but current social and institutional changes are clearly pointing in that direction. Overall, the participation of women in higher education is now close to matching that of men, and mature students are increasingly entering the system to further and update previously broken educational careers.

The pressure on higher education to become 'responsive' to the more immediate economic needs of the labour market has increased, as has demands on 'accountability' in terms of curricular quality, teaching efficiency and students' labour-market outcomes. The issue of 'vocationalism' in higher education has been one of the items in the forefront of debates about the costs and consequences of the changing nature of higher education and its student body. Graduates from institutions in higher education can no longer be seen to constitute an elite, whose educational needs and quality, cultural status, employability and future economic security can be taken for granted. There is and will increasingly continue to be a decline in commonality between students both in what they bring with them to higher education in terms of background credentials, and what can be expected of them when they leave. This expansion of higher education seems increasingly likely to be accompanied by a movement away from a centrally directed system towards a more market-oriented approach to students and courses, which will mean that the nature of student demand will be an important determinant of how institutions determine their individual policy for course provision. We can anticipate more, rather than less diversity in the future, a diversity increasingly based as much on social demand as on labour-market needs (Williams 1989; Brennan and Jarry 1991). As it is the polytechnic and colleges of higher education which have done most to extend access to higher education for new categories of students, there is some justification for looking in some detail at the experiences and perceptions of the students in this group of institutions.

Concurrent with this recent expansion in British higher education has been important labour-market changes for UK graduates. Graduates no longer enter a range of narrowly defined elite professions, but a much expanded and increasingly differentiated and segmented labour market, where a range of occupations not previously in the 'graduate sector' has moved 'up' with accompanying demands on the nature of educational credentials. The needs in all areas of the economy for highly educated and skilled labour is growing, but especially in the areas of engineering, computing and finance. There is also a growing shortage of teachers in the areas of science, technology and mathematics. But the growth in labour-market opportunities is not confined to these areas, but cover a much wider field of managerial and professional occupations. This increase in demand for graduates relates both to occupations and industries where graduates are recruited primarily for their specialist skills, and to those in which they are recruited primarily for their more general abilities. It is noted by one recent report on the graduate labour market that one of the largest areas of employment growth along with that for science and technology graduates, is expected to be for those qualified in the social sciences (CIHE 1988; Pearson and Pike 1989; DES 1990; Wilson et al. 1990).

Though both the changing manpower needs of the economy and increasing social demand have contributed to the growth and diversification of higher education, those two factors are not always in harmony with each other. One of the problems to which this gives rise is the failure of social demand to adjust to particular changing manpower needs and shortages in the economy as they arise in specific areas of sometimes temporary, sometimes long-term growth. There is what has been termed a 'mismatch' or a 'lag' between the outcomes of higher-education and employer requirements. This has especially affected technologically oriented subjects, jobs and professions in areas such as engineering and computing. A further aspect of this 'mismatch' has been seen to be the changing skills needs of graduate jobs in general, resulting from a transformation of work organisation and processes especially at management levels, and the kinds of qualities fostered by higher-education courses (Mabey 1986). Special concerns have been expressed by employers about student competencies in the area of numerical application, as in, for example, financial management, and the use and application of 'new technology'. The problem for both higher education and employers is here two fold. Firstly, how can students, especially other than school leavers, be attracted to courses in shortage areas; and secondly, how can students on all courses be given such general skills as to make graduates more vocationally flexible and to facilitate substitution in the labour market as new needs arise? During the recession in the early 1980s it was often assumed that higher rates of unemployment amongst graduates from particular subject areas, such as humanities and social sciences, would gradually, once labour market information filtered down through the system, lead to a shift of students away from these areas. Such a shift does on the whole not appear to have taken place, nor does it look likely to do so in the near future.

The decline in the number of students applying to study engineering and technology subjects in the universities has been marked over the last few years. With the expansion of the polytechnics, these institutions have fared better in this respect and show some growth in the numbers of students graduating in the areas of science and technology (Pearson and Pike 1989). Growth in maths and computing, an area of polytechnic strength, accounts for a large part of this expansion. But if we look at the nature of student enrolment, we see that not only is a very large proportion of engineering and technology students in the polytechnics on part-time courses in comparison to the universities, the overall number of such students is considerably smaller than the numbers of students enrolled on courses in business studies and social sciences, both full-time and part-time, and on other 'liberal arts' courses (Ball 1989). Are students not getting the message? Some findings from the HELM project can throw some light on this.

Firstly, and most importantly, graduates do get jobs. A couple of years into employment there are no major subject differences in employment rates, though there are subject differences in the ease and speed with which employment is gained, and in the proportion of students that go through a period of post-graduate study in advance of seeking a job, as well as in the proportion of graduates not actively seeking work for personal or family reasons. Graduates seeking work get it (Brennan and McGeevor 1988; Lyon, McGeevor and Murray 1988). Secondly, there is evidence that graduates, when asked about the main benefits looked for in higher education, irrespective of subject field, place almost equal emphasis on personal development and subject interest as on employment prospects, and often use higher education in itself as a period in which to discover and define their career aims. In other words, many students do not enter higher education with financially attractive immediate employment as the overriding goal. The HELM research projects have isolated three broad categories of relationships between courses and the labour market: courses offering 'occupational specialisms', where the content of the course aims to prepare students for a particular job (e.g. engineer or systems analyst); courses with an intermediate vocational relevance aiming for more general links with a particular area of employment (e.g. business studies or social administration); and a third category of 'generalist' programmes of study not directly linked to any particular kind of employment but leading to jobs where recruitment is based on general skills, competencies and dispositions rather than specific expertise (e.g. general social science courses, arts and humanities) (Silver and Brennan 1988).

There is, as has been noted above, a proven demand in the labour market for graduates from the last course type. In other words, for students not wishing to enter vocationally well defined courses, or courses in specialist subject areas in high demand, such as engineering and computing, there are still interesting graduate jobs to be had at the end, albeit after a slightly longer wait and with somewhat lower incomes. Nor is it always the case that having a vocationally relevant degree in high demand in itself will be sufficient to gain a job with speed and ease, since such factors as type of graduating institution, social class, gender, and ethnicity will often be of equal importance in determining who gets a 'good' job (Gatley 1988; Chapman 1988; Boys and Kirkland 1988; Brennan and McGeevor 1988).

When finally, as will be discussed below, the path into technologically oriented disciplines typically demands background credentials of a kind and a level which a large proportion of students wishing to enter higher education do not possess nor can easily afford to get, gaining such pre-entry qualifications must, in the light of the above, seem a hurdle too arduous to have to jump in the first place. An interesting business studies, social sciences or humanities degree offering personal and social development as well as some general educational skills, becomes an option which is as 'rational' as it is attractive.

RECRUITMENT AND ADMISSIONS

If the curriculum and its implementation can be described as the 'secret garden' of educational establishments, then the admissions process is the 'secret gate' in the back wall of that garden. Access to higher education in Britain is expanding, but it is by no means open (Fulton 1988). The process of selection that enters into the recruitment process in higher education is complex and interacts with the educational and vocational expectations and aspirations of students. These aspirations are both guided and circumscribed by the various entry standards, both formal and informal, that are laid down by institutions, course teams and professional regulatory bodies in competition with each other for both student quality and numbers. Courses and subjects in high demand amongst prospective students can operate a greater selectivity on the basis of educational criteria, than those where student demand is high amongst students with more mixed educational backgrounds and lower-quality credentials. The system of recruitment is not only diversified, it is also hierarchical, both between subjects and courses, as well as between different types of institutions. When there is a drop in demand for a particular subject, entry standards need to be lowered if the same number of students are to be admitted, as has been observed is presently happening to engineering (THES 31.8.90). When the demand is high, entry standards need to be increased, unless some system of 'targets' or informal 'quotas' are set to accommodate a particular group of students seen to be important for recruitment, such as women, mature students or members of local minority groups.

In the polytechnics, this has been the case on many courses in the human sciences. With no *common* entrance prerequisite or exam for entry to higher education, it is in practice up to each course team to define the parameters within which individual 'portfolios' of credentials will be acceptable for entry. With the A-level qualification itself narrow and discipline based, accepting candidates with few A-level qualifications is necessary and common. As the ability to attract especially mature students has become a performance indicator for many higher-education establishments, this has in the last decade resulted in a proliferation of so call 'access' courses offering a more study-skills-oriented educational preparation for a specific subject area in higher education, such as social sciences, law, or biotechnology, sometimes specifically tailor made for an individual degree programme. Both school leavers and mature students coming from work or from further education colleges, work out for themselves 'packages' of credentials that they need and are prepared to seek for the sake of entry to particular courses and institutions. Such educational strategies are often worked out in consultation with teachers, parents, careers officers and other parties involved in the process of helping to facilitate as straight forward as possible an entry to higher education. For students without financial resources, this, as well as academic abilities and inclinations, becomes an important factor in the decision making about which credentials to seek and the time to be spent in preparing for entry to higher education. There is a well established relationship between social class and A-level performance, with students from the higher echelons of society gaining more and higher-quality A-levels, and thus a more general educational background than students doing only one or two A-levels in particular subjects.

It is beyond the confines of this paper to discuss the many issues raised by the uneven distribution between men and women of types of secondary-school qualifications and its implications for subject choice. The stark difference in educational credentials between boys and girls starts early (Chapman 1988). The new core curriculum, it is hoped, will change this for future generations of boys and girls, but for mature women recruits to higher education some form of 'compensatory' education in mathematics, computing and sciences would be essential to enable them to enter any areas of technology, either old or 'new'. Compensatory education programmes cost money, and as mature women in search of higher education on the whole do not command either time or financial resources, and are not in a position to accumulate loans, expecting them to finance themselves through longer periods of study is unrealistic. What are seen to be 'easier' and quicker options than the return to numeracy and science will prevail. The outcome of this in choice of subject to study in higher education is clear (Table 12.1). The absence of women on engineering courses is very marked. (For the 1985 cohort of graduates studied, the sample had to be 'weighted' to include enough women graduates in some areas in the study to enable meaningful gender comparisons). Looking at qualification requirements alone, there is little hope that mature women will be able to seek entry to technology and engineering courses or related subjects without major resources being put into preparatory education and student grants.

Table 12.1 Comparison of degree subjects taken

Degree subject taken	Men (%)	Women (%)
Modern languages	20.0	80.0
English literature	23.6	76.4
Psychology	27.7	72.3
Humanities	39.9	60.1
Applied chemistry	83.6	16.4
Electrical & electronic engineering	98.1	1.9
Civil engineering	98.5	1.5
Production engineering	100.0	0.0
All subjects	53.1	46.9

The effect on course choice of differing qualification demands between different courses is also important for mature students, i.e. students who enter at 21 or older, many of whom do not possess standard A-level qualifications. For the 1985 HELM sample, a comparison was made between the average A-level points of students on the courses in the sample. There is a notable diversity between subjects and institutions in the educational background of their students. Universities are overall able to command a much higher profile of entry requirements than polytechnics in the same subject areas. The much higher proportion of mature students on courses in polytechnics may partly account for this difference (Table 12.2) and for the growth in the number of engineering and technology students in polytechnics relative to the universities.

Table 12.2 Comparison of entry requirements (% of students in the 1985 cohort)

	Six or more A-level points		Nine or more A-level points	
Subject	University (%)	Polytechnic (%)	University (%)	Polytechnic (%)
Economics	95	45		
Biology	92	23	79	6
Mechanical engineering	74	25	63	8
Computing	71	43	47	12

Moreover, it can be seen that competitive demand for places is as important a determinant of standards required than the nature of the course itself, in that general science courses, biology and mechanical engineering in polytechnics have lower A-level scores than subjects such as performing arts and modern languages. Courses popular with mature students and with women are on the whole, however, those 'easier' to gain entry to, such as social sciences and humanities. Students who for various reasons opted out of doing maths and science at O and A-level, or who completed secondary school with only one to two weak A-levels, have already before they enter higher education been excluded from a whole range of courses and occupations. The selective, specialised and – from a social class point of view – strongly elitist nature of present secondary education in Britain, closes doors very early for some pupils and has particularly detrimental effects on the possibilities of growth in higher education in areas requiring a broad background in science and numeracy (Ball, 1989).

In view of the increasing market orientation of higher education funding, courses will continue to be under pressure to recruit as many students as institutions can hold. With demand high from students without the necessary prerequisites for the study of science and technology, institutions will, all things being equal, have to continue to support courses in non-technological subject areas. They will also increasingly have to enter into closer liaisons with further-education colleges to ensure the provision of prerequisites in science and mathematics to attract students away from non-technological areas, a difficult, costly and time-consuming task. The question that arises is the extent to which potential 'new' kinds of recruits into higher education would be prepared and motivated to attend qualifying, adequately designed courses in science and mathematics, if a place on a degree course or a job can be gained without it.

WHAT IS HIGHER EDUCATION FOR?

With rising social demand for higher education as well as labour-market demands calling the tune on course provision, student educational aspirations and labour-market orientations become important factors to consider in the making of higher education policy. Further, with growing proportions of mature entrants, students will increasingly have to be viewed as 'consumers' and 'clients', whose perceived needs and wishes have to be considered, even though these may at times be in conflict with those of employers as the 'users' of their skills. As the HELM research has shown, students are not automatically drawn in the first instance to courses with immediate and attractive employment opportunities. The potential advantage of a degree depends on a student's 'starting position', both educationally and from a status point of view, and on the student's more general personal aspirations for the future (Brennan and McGeevor 1988; Boys and Kirkland 1988). There is a shared emphasis on a wide range of satisfactions arising from degree study, in which good income and status, though important, are by no means the only or even primary objectives. The growing demand for higher education can only in part be explained in terms of goals defined by the labour market. It is also about more diffuse issues of personal development and satisfactions, sometimes with the expressed purpose of deferring career decisions till after completing the course. General economic incentives may guide the pursuit of higher education in general, in that graduates gain better employment opportunities and are awarded higher incomes at the end than those earned by non-graduates, but individuals also study for other reasons. The degree to which students choose a course for career-related reasons varies between different courses. Students from more 'generalist' subjects such as humanities, social sciences and modern languages are less likely to see their choice of subject as career and job related, than students from more vocationally defined and 'specialist' subject areas such as computing, electrical engineering and accountancy. 'Generalist' subject areas are also where more women and mature graduates are to be found, and where there are lower entry qualification hurdles to compete with.

International comparative studies of higher education and the labour market point to the desire among many students for a 'broad' approach to higher education and its relation to career aspirations that allows intrinsic as well as extrinsic values to be pursued. When presented with a choice between studying a subject they find interesting, or studying a subject offering good future career prospects, most students opt for the former possibility. There is agreement in studies that whichever way orientations are looked at, students in some subject areas such as vocational courses in commercial subjects, engineering and law, show a greater propensity for extrinsic, pragmatic and materialistic values than students of humanities, social sciences and arts for whom more intrinsic rewards stand out as important. This is so despite a shared knowledge and understanding of the relative financial position of various occupational groups in the labour market (Sanyal 1987; Boys and Kirkland 1988). It has also been shown that students entering higher education from non-traditional educational routes, as well as women and working-class students, are less motivated by specific occupational considerations than male school leavers, and are in general at present to be found in degree subjects where employment prospects are less immediately favourable for all graduates, such as arts and social sciences (other than business studies) (Redpath and Harvey 1987; Tarsh 1989).

The HELM data on graduate attitudes allow for the exploration of the notion of student 'orientation' a bit further, in order to isolate clusters of factors that enter into motivations which enables us to relate these clusters to the chosen subject of study and to student character-istics. Graduates were asked a range of questions directed at the occupa-tional orientations and self-perceptions of graduates in particular subject areas. They were asked to indicate the importance of a series of items to their choice of a long-term job, and to mark the importance of various spheres of life to them, as well as to give an indication of how they thought of themselves. Factor analysis of these sets of questions allows the isolation of different orientation types, three of which will here be discussed: 'careerist', 'inner-directed', and 'altruistic' work orientations. The factor labelled 'careerist' was show to correlate strongly with items such as 'a strong possibility of rapid promotion', 'high prestige and social status', 'high salary', 'job security', 'opportunity for professional development' and 'the chance to exercise leadership'. The highest scor-ers on this factor were shown to be courses of a vocational nature such as production engineering, pharmacy, business studies and accountancy. It is interesting to note that maths, computing and other engineering and science subjects are not as attractive to students with a careerist orientation as law, a traditional high-status, high-income occupation. The least 'careerist' are graduates in fine art, environmental science, English literature and humanities. The 'inner-directed work orientation' factor strongly correlates with the following: 'the opportunity to be creative', 'the opportunity to use one's special skills and abilities', 'rela-tive freedom from supervision from others' and 'work that is continually challenging'. It is perhaps not surprising to find the art and design graduates showing a more 'inner-directed' orientation. At the other extreme are the graduates in maths, law, science and economics, who are more concerned with financial and careerist rewards. Finally, the 'atruistic' orientation is defined by a high correlation with items such as 'opportunity to help others', 'potential for improving society', 'oppor-tunity to work with people'. The subject areas included in the survey where the greatest proportion of 'altruistically' oriented students were to be found are nursing, pharmacy, psychology and humanities. Courses scoring the least on 'altruism' were shown to be business studies, maths, production engineering and urban estate management. Only in the case of pharmacy, does the search for a financially rewarding career appear to go hand in hand with a desire for an altruistic contribution through work.

So, for a variety of reasons to do both with the nature of the labour market and with individual wishes and desires, courses attract students with different kinds of orientations to the future. Courses send different 'signals' to students about the kinds of labour market orientation they foster. How does this affect which kinds of students they are capable of attracting? The orientations discussed above are not unrelated to the educational status of such courses as regards entry standards, or to the 'social catchment' of a course. Students with a 'careerist' orientation are on courses where average entry qualifications are higher and more selective. It is beyond the scope of this chapter to discuss the question of what comes first, the motivation or the required credentials, but whatever the nature of this interaction, by the point of entry to higher education the consequences of this interaction is already apparent and the strong relationship between age, gender, social class, educational qualifications and occupational aspirations well established. As we might expect the potential 'new' recruits to higher education and into technologically based subjects, mature students, working-class students and women are not only characterised by inadequate pre-higher-education qualifications, they may also lack the motivation in large numbers to pursue such subject areas. Mature graduates in the 1982 sample expressed more of an 'inner-directed orientation' to work than standard entrants, who were more 'careerist' in their approach. For many mature candidates, returning to study is about improving the quality of life at work as much as about gaining career advantages. Again, predictably, women in the sample were shown to express a more 'altruistic' work orientation than the men, who were more 'careerist'. This 'altruistic' orientation of women to their future needs is not unrelated to a realistic assessment that 'altruism' in their own home and to their own children necessitates a work environment sympathetic to the needs of care and carers, all too rare in industry (Metcalfe 1990). It was also shown to be the case that graduates from working- and lower middle-class backgrounds expressed less of a 'careerist' orientation, than students from the higher echelons of society. It may be that students from a background without a tradition in higher education are looking for more general and personally developmental cultural gains, and a route out of lower-grade work.

Much has been written about the absence in British cultural history of a scientific and technological tradition, the lack of an 'industrial spirit' and an absence of faith in the intellectual excitements and fruits of technology. The notion of being 'cultured' in Britain does not include the ability to count, build a stereo set, or conduct an experiment. It does include the ability to be discursive in words and speech, awareness of literature and politics, a humanistic social conscience and confidence in self-presentation. For students in search of personal development and intrinsic or altruistic rewards from life and work, neither a 'careerist' vocational and labour-market-oriented approach, nor the pursuit of a specialist technologically oriented curriculum look very likely to deliver the goods. One can only conclude with the thought that whatever compensatory educational ventures are offered to potential new recruits in the areas of maths, science and technology to enable them to pursue careers in these fields, potential students will have to be motivated to join such ventures and to wish to stay on and bring the fruits of their hard work into the labour market. As many pupils in school and students in further education have already avoided what are seen as demanding subject areas in favour of more immediately attractive options, quick 'conversions' will not come easily and not without a great deal more financial and economic support both from the government, higher education and employers.

A GENERALLY COMPETENT GRADUATE?

For a student who enters higher education without an educational background broad enough either to encompass sufficient mathematics, science and technology to enter specialist courses, or to enable easy later 'conversion', what does the higher education curriculum do to help? Conversely, for students entering technologically oriented courses, how well are they serviced in the common search for a more general cultural and personally developmental education? Not very well it seems. The recent debate on 'transferable skills' and general 'competencies' in higher education has highlighted problems with generic and personal skills training in the higher education curriculum. Such skills have been seen to cover three areas of competencies: communication skills (both written and oral), social skills (such as team work and leadership ability) and general intellectual problem-solving skills as fostered in mathematics, computing and the sciences. From the point of view of employers, such basic skills being common to many graduate jobs, should be taught outside any particular industry or profession in schools and colleges, and constitute part of what makes a graduate 'employable' (Bradshaw 1985). As argued above, such skills can be seen to be part of what in the sociology of education has come to be referred to as 'cultural capital', and it can safely be assumed that students from financially and educationally more favoured backgrounds are more likely to possess such general skills upon entry to higher education than most of Britain's mature entrants to higher education. For others, successful schooling should, it can be argued, operate as a 'compensatory' mechanism for the fostering of such skills. The UK Educational Reform Act of 1988, with its introduction of a National Curriculum core for primary and secondary schools, has had as one of its aims both to broaden and to sharpen such general skills training for everyone not only in its emphasis on the three 'R's, but also in its focus on a wider range of compulsory subjects and on skills integrated subjects such as crafts, design and technology. The National Curriculum core is intended to make it difficult for schools to let particular categories of pupils 'slip through' by dropping out of particular subject areas too soon, for example, girls out of maths and science (Flude and Hammer 1989). But many entry cohorts of mature students will continue to remain untouched by these reforms.

During debates on transferable skills in higher education, much discussion has taken place as to the extent to which the fostering of such broad general skills is also the responsibility of higher education, and on how this responsibility ought to be exercised. Does, as has been argued by some academics, the experience of higher education itself, the day-to-day work in labs, seminars, workshops and tutorials in themselves provide such skills as a positive but accidental by-product, a 'happy coincidence', to subject learning, or does a higher education in expansion have to begin to look more constructively at what ought to go into a continuing common core curriculum for undergraduates? (Bradshaw 1985; Lyon 1988).

Evidence from the HELM surveys points to key areas of concern regarding the higher education curriculum, areas which have a direct bearing on the relationship between higher education and the fostering of technical knowledge and development. I have already discussed the general variety and individual narrowness of students' educational backgrounds on different courses, especially as regards maths and science, and A-level point scores. Using the graduates themselves as 'course evaluators', there is also a clear variability between courses in the extent to which students feel they have been given opportunities to develop further particular areas of skills. Both the 1982 and the 1985 samples were asked whether their experience of higher education had helped them in a range of what albeit vaguely, can be described as general 'competencies'. A considerable amount of consensus was shown on several abilities, with general intellectual skills such as 'ability to think critically', to 'act independently', to 'organise one's own work' and to 'apply new knowledge', perceived by all graduates to have been considerably improved by the higher-education experience whatever subject studied. These are all abilities which most students would pick up 'on the way', simply by spending time in a traditional academic environment.

There were, however, other potential benefits on which there was a great deal less agreement between students on different courses. These were more practical benefits such as 'written and spoken communication' and the 'ability to handle numerical data'. The evidence points to the persistence in British education and culture of the great divide between what has come to be called the 'two cultures'. The graduate panel shows that computing, science and engineering graduates feel that they have only gained a small amount as regards the abilities of written and spoken communications, abilities which students in social sciences and humanities feel they have had better fostered. In their study of engineering courses, Silver and Brennan point to the curricular difficulties faced by such courses in trying to squeeze in both general and specific skills and knowledge in a short three-year time span (Silver and Brennan 1988). Some of the more personal skills development in communication suffers as a result, which may be a factor detracting from the attractiveness of such courses for students in search of a more general personally developmental education.

When we get to the 'ability to handle numerical data', the subject-related nature of this ability, whatever it may mean to individual graduates, stands out most strongly. In comparison to the ability to think critically, which all graduates feel gets encouraged, numeracy is the one ability with the greatest deviation across subjects, and the one that least fits the pattern of a 'general ability' improved by the experience of higher education itself. Students without numerate backgrounds who enter courses where qualifications in numeracy, or qualifications presuming skills in numeracy, are not a prerequisite for entry, are able to perpetuate the gap in their knowledge through higher education and into the labour market. It is also the case that a high proportion of students on 'non-numerate' courses in the HELM samples expressed the view that they had been given insufficient opportunities for the development of skills in computing and numeracy, and, conversely, students in science and engineering courses would have liked to have had opportunities to develop further their skills in written and oral communications (Brennan and McGeevor 1988). The 'two cultures' operate inside the higher-education curriculum as well as outside it. With worsening staff – student ratios and a shrinking unit of resource in higher education, attempts to widen the curricular offer across this cultural divide are not likely to come from course teams struggling to keep up the basics of discipline standards.

CONCLUSION: TOWARDS A MORE GENERAL HIGHER EDUCATION FOR ALL

Over the next decades both graduate employers and higher education are going to have to find mechanisms with which to adapt to the changing nature of the students' body in an expanding higher education. The present growth in the variety and flexibility of curricula on offer in higher education, both as regards entry requirements and course contents not only within but also between institutions, will enable a wider variety of British adults and school leavers to feel motivated to develop and explore their individual educational interests and occupational needs. With the graduate labour market growing in all fields, students will not be short of labour-market opportunities at the end, whatever field they choose to enter. But the benefits of the expansion for the growth and development of technology and related areas, in teaching and research as well as in industry appears more doubtful. It is difficult not to conclude that a major rethink is necessary, both of the structure and content of further and higher education to enable more students to become technologically literate, and of the way in which employers and the labour market define work opportunities and careers to make them more attractive to a wider catchment of students than young men. With A-level reform slow in coming and with mature students, especially women, and lower-class school leavers with a narrower range of secondary-school qualifications the major sources of expansion in higher education, the need for a fresh look at the undergraduate curriculum as a whole seems inevitable.

In an article on transferable skills, Bradshaw notes that the response of higher education in Britain to employer needs has been more in the development of subject specialists and degrees of vocationalism than in the fostering of generic skills in programmes of 'general education' capable of transformation into a variety of both personal, civic and vocational abilities (Bradshaw 1985). He contrasts this situation with that of higher education in the US, where some form of 'core' of general education has been part of the undergraduate curriculum for a long time with first-degree programmes combining a core of general education with in-depth specialist study. With a high proportion of its population in higher education, general education of both knowledge and skills has not in the US been taken as pre-determined and given by the school system, but has been seen as an intrinsic part of what should go into the curriculum until the post-graduate stage. Vocational specialisation into varieties of graduate professions is seen to lie more in post-graduate, than in undergraduate education. It is important to note that such a concept of general education is not to be confused with what in British higher education used to be called 'liberal studies', a minor curricular input on science and engineering courses designed to 'humanise' and 'civilise' such students beyond the confines of their narrow disciplines. A general undergraduate core curriculum is also designed to include requirements for the teaching of basic science, technology and numeracy for students choosing to specialise in the human science. Such a core curriculum gives all students access to the kinds of skills and topics that many students in search of a 'broad' education are after. It also, perhaps more reluctantly, gives all students as a matter of course, access to the very basics of science, numeracy and technology. It postpones 'enforced' specialisation for those still in search of their futures, and offers specialist opportunities both during and after undergraduate studies.

But neither curricular reform, nor changes in labour-market work practices in the areas of scientific and technological development will happen without a major input of financial resources. The teaching of science and technology, at whatever level it is done, is expensive. With higher education establishments competing with each other for scarce resources and scarce students, and students increasingly forced to carry the cost themselves, 'easy' and 'cheap' options are more likely to prevail. Everything else being equal, I can foresee an even larger number of students flocking to do subjects in the human sciences in the future, and polytechnics and universities thankful to squeeze them in.

References

Acker, S. and Warren Piper, D. (eds) (1984), *Is Higher Education Fair to Women?*, Surrey, SHRE/NFER-Nelson.

Ball, C. (1989), *Aim Higher: widening access to higher education*, (Interim Report for the Education/Industry Forum's Higher Education Steering Group, RSA/Industry Matters, London.

Boys, C. and Kirkland, J. (1988), *Degrees of Success*, London, Jessica Kingsley.

Bradshaw, D. (1985), 'Transferable intellectual and personal skills', *Oxford Review of Education*, 11(2).

Brennan, J. and McGeevor, P. (1988), *Graduates at Work*, London, Jessica Kingsley.

Brennan, J. and Jarry, D. (eds) (1991), *Degrees of Inequality*, London, Jessica Kingsley.

Chapman, T. (1988), *Just the Ticket: graduate men and women in the labour market three years after leaving college*, HELM Working Paper no. 8, North Staffordshire Polytechnic, Stoke-on-Trent.

Council for Industry and Higher Education (1988), *Towards a Partnership: Higher Education. Government. Industry*, London, CIHE.

DES (1990) *Highly Qualified People: supply and demand*, (Report on an Interdepartmental Review), London, HMSO.

Flude, M. and Hammer, M. (eds) (1989), *The Education Reform Act 1988*, London, Falmer Press.

Fulton, O. (1988), 'Elite survivals? Entry "standards" and procedures for higher education admissions', *Studies in Higher Education*, 13(1).

Gatley, D. A. (1988), 'The influence of social-class origins on the choice of course career preferences, and entry to employment of CNAA graduates', PH.D. thesis, North Staffordshire Polytechnic, Stoke-on-Trent.

Gordon, A. (1983) 'Attitudes of employers to the recruitment of graduates', *Education Studies*, 9.

Lyon, E. S. (1988), *Academic Abilities and Transferable Skills: a discussion*, HELM Working Paper 7, London, South Bank Polytechnic.

Lyon, E. S., McGeevor, P. and Murray, K. (1988), *After Higher Education: the experience of a sample of 1985 graduates and diplomates two years after graduation*, HELM publication, London, South Bank Polytechnic.

Lyon, E. S. and Murray, K. (1992) 'Graduate labour markets and the new vocationalism in higher education', in G. Payne and M. Cross (eds), *Sociology in Action*, London, Macmillan.

Mabey, C. (1986), *Graduates into Industry*, London, Gower.

Metcalfe, Hilary (1990), *Retaining Women Employees: measures to counteract labour shortages*, IMS report no. 190, Brighton, Institute of Manpower Studies.

Morgan, W. J. and Scott, N. T. (1987), *Unemployed Graduates: a wasted national resource*, Nottingham, University of Nottingham, Centre of Labour and Management Studies.

Pearson, R. and Pike, G. (1989), *The Graduate Labour Market in the 1990s*, IMS Report no. 167, Brighton, Institute of Manpower Studies.

Redpath, B. and Harvey, B. (1987), *Young People's Intention to Enter Higher Education*, Office of Population Census and Surveys, London, HMSO.

Roizen, J. and Jepson, M. (1985), *Degrees for Jobs: employer expectations of higher education*, Guildford, SRHE/NFER-Nelson.

Sanyal, B. C. (1987), *Higher Education and Employment*, London, Falmer Press.

Silver, H. and Brennan, J. (1988), *A Liberal Vocationalism*, London, Methuen.

Tarsh, J. (1989), 'New graduate destinations by age of graduation', *Employment Gazette*, November.

Times Higher Educational Supplement (1990), 'Engineering lowers the odds to successful entry', 31 August.

Williams, G. (1985), 'Graduate employment and vocationalism in higher education', *European Journal of Education* 20(2–3).

Williams, G. (1989), 'Higher Education', in M. Flude and M. Hammer (eds), *The Education Reform Act 1988*, London, Falmer Press.

Wilson, R. A., Bosworth, D. L. and Taylor, P. T. (1990), *Projecting the Labour Market for the Highly Qualified*, Coventry, Institute of Employment Research, University of Warwick.

Index